I0815241

POCKET PRAYERS FOR

HILLARY MORGAN FERRER

with JULIE LOOS

HARVEST HOUSE PUBLISHERS

EUGENE, OREGON

Scripture versions used can be found in the back of this book.

Cover design by Bryce Williamson

Cover images © HappyPanda789, UfimtsevaV / Getty Images

Interior design by Angie Renich, Wildwood Digital Publishing

For bulk, special sales, or ministry purchases, please call 1-800-547-8979.
Email: CustomerService@hhpbooks.com

Pocket Prayers for Mama Bears is an abridged edition of *Honest Prayers for Mama Bears* by Hillary Morgan Ferrer with Julie Loos.

Pocket Prayers for Mama Bears

Published by Harvest House Publishers
Eugene, Oregon 97408
www.harvesthousepublishers.com

ISBN 978-0-7369-9077-6 (hardcover)
ISBN 978-0-7369-9078-3 (eBook)

Library of Congress Control Number: 2022945900

Printed in China

24 25 26 27 28 29 30 31 32 33 / RDS / 10 9 8 7 6 5 4 3 2 1

Hillary:

This book is for all the Mama Bears who have bought into the lie that their prayers need to be eloquent. They don't. My desire is that this book sets you free from the self-condemning voice that discourages you from coming to God because you think you're "not good at prayer." Nah. Just say it all, Mama Bears, and then turn toward the truth of His Word. Everyone has to start somewhere.

Julie:

To my paternal grandmother, Henrietta "Tom" Dalton, who modeled what it meant to be a praying woman and prayed for me more than I will ever know. To my first grandchild, Anna Ruth Loos, and my future grandchildren, whom I promise to pray for, and to my daughters-in-law Mary and Sarah as they become praying Mama Bears. To my Lord and Savior, Jesus Christ, who intercedes for me.

Contents

1. Beginning Prayer: Raising Dragon Slayers in an Era of Dragons 11

Section 1: Selfless Prayers for Self

2. Craving for the Word 15
3. Eternal Perspective 16
4. Wise Use of Money 17
5. Give Me a Moldable Heart 18
6. Self-Discipline 20
7. A Life of Balance and Discernment 22
8. Stewarding My Body Well 24
9. Prayer over Blind Spots 26

Section 2: Spiritual Protection for the Home Turf

10. Bedroom 29
11. Kids' Bedrooms 30
12. Living Room 31
13. The Digital Sphere 32
14. Kitchen 34
15. Grandparents' House 35
16. Child's Friend's House 37

Section 3: From Bzzzz!!! to Zzzzz...
Short Prayers for the Daily Grind

17. Upon Waking Up ... 41
18. Prayer from Head to Toes ... 42
19. Blessing over Quiet Time ... 43
20. Before the Tasks I Don't Enjoy ... 44
21. Preparing to Reengage with Kids ... 45
22. Before Watching Entertainment ... 46
23. Before Putting Kids to Bed ... 47
24. Release at the End of the Day ... 48

Section 4: Ages, Stages, and Rhythms of Life

25. To Not Screw Up My Toddler ... 51
26. Children Exploring Independence ... 52
27. For a Child with Separation Anxiety ... 53
28. Blessing over Children on Their Birthdays ... 54
29. School Decision ... 56
30. Pubescent Identity Crisis ... 58
31. Releasing My Almost-Adult Children ... 60
32. Adult Children to Walk Faithfully with God ... 61

Section 5: From Clay to Vessel
Prayers for My Kids' Spiritual Formation

33. Child's Salvation ... 65
34. Child to Develop Personal Faith ... 66
35. Kids to Love the Word ... 67
36. For Children to Love the Church ... 68

37. Fostering Gratitude and Contentment 70
38. Healthy Outlets for Emotions 71
39. When Kid Makes a Big Mistake 73
40. Discerning God's Voice from Other Voices 74
41. For Child's Sin to Be Exposed 75
42. Reconciliation and Forgiveness When Hurt 77
43. Cultivating Sexual Faithfulness 78

Section 6: Things My Kids Have to Deal With

44. Stewarding Popularity Well 83
45. Dealing with Rejection 84
46. When My Child Feels Alone in Following Christ 85
47. Good Friends for My Son 87
48. Good Friends for My Daughter 89
49. Nightmares 91
50. Dating 92
51. Teenagers with Raging Hormones 94
52. Pressure to Fit In 96
53. Protection Against Comparison 97
54. Broken Hearts 98

Section 7: Welcome to the Rumbllllllle

55. When I Have Been Wronged (and Want to Release the Kraken) 101
56. Before Engaging in Conflict Resolution 103
57. Loving the Unlovable 104
58. When Everyone Is at Each Other's Throat 105

59. Parenting the Children I Have (and Releasing Who I Think They Should Be) 106
60. Calming Down Before Disciplining My Child 108
61. Asking for My Child's Forgiveness 109
62. When I Really Don't Like Someone but Want To ... 111
63. Establishing Boundaries with Toxic Family Members 113

Section 8: Does This Prayer Make Me Look Fat?

64. When I Just Want to Pee Alone 117
65. When Social Media Has Warped My View of Motherhood 118
66. When My Mouth Gets Me in Trouble 120
67. Unhealthy Fixations 121
68. Prayer over Habitual Sin 122
69. When I'm Too Comfortable with a Shallow Faith 123
70. When I Don't Understand Prayer 125
71. When I Feel Like I Have Let God Down 126

Section 9: When. I. Just. Can't. Even.

72. Courage for Being Misunderstood as a Christian ... 131
73. Longing for Justice in an Unjust World 133
74. Loving like Jesus When the World Has Redefined Love 135
75. When My Kids Are So Loud, Needy, and Whiny That I Want to Scream 137
76. When I Want to Run Away from My Responsibilities 139

77. Am I Doing Enough? 140
78. When I Feel like the Wrong Mom for the Job 141
79. Praying Through Exhaustion 142
80. Asking the Holy Spirit to Help Me Pray 144
81. When God Feels Silent 146
82. God, Please Use a Megaphone 147
83. When My Anxiety About the World Rubs Off on My Child 149
84. When I Can't Focus on My Bible Reading 151

Section 10: Mind, Body, and Emotions

85. Healthy Attitude Toward My Body 155
86. Taming Emotions 157
87. When My Brain Needs to Slow the Heck Down 158
88. General Healing 160
89. Anxiety-Ridden Child 161

Section 11: Church, State, School, and Culture

90. For Our Churches to Become Healthier 165
91. For Unity and Division 167
92. For Biblically Minded Teachers and Administrators in Public School 169
93. Protection for Teachers Who Refuse to Teach Lies 171
94. Protection over Freedom of Speech and Religion in Schools 172
95. When My Child Is Bullied 174
96. When My Child Is the Bully 176

97. Atmosphere in the Traditional Classroom 178
98. Atmosphere While Homeschooling............... 180
99. Child's Ability to Learn/Learning Disabilities 182
100. Ending Prayer: Creating a Legacy of Prayer 184
Answered Prayer Requests 185

Beginning Prayer:
Raising Dragon Slayers in an Era of Dragons

Jennifer DeFrates

Dear Lord, I am scared for my children growing up in a world that celebrates sinfulness and bombards them with flawed and deceptive definitions of love, identity, and truth. Please strengthen me as a parent and believer. Grant me wisdom so I may raise my children to think biblically and rationally through every issue they will face. Give me the courage to lovingly speak truth when our world distorts what Your Word says about our bodies, minds, behaviors, and beliefs. Make me wise enough to know when to be silent and brave enough to know when to speak.

Show me how to raise my children to see the image of God in all people, treating them as immortal souls God has designed and created for a purpose. Let the Holy Spirit work through me to demonstrate Your perfect grace and mercy so that my children see what it looks like to love others well. Open doors for me to share the gospel often in front of my children. I don't want to be a Christian in name only. Help me protect and nurture my children's hearts and minds while inoculating them against culture's lies.

Lastly, Lord, I beg You to work within my children. Create a strong faith in them. Help them to know You personally and have their own faith and convictions. Give me peace knowing that You will carry them through anything if they lean into deep fellowship with You. Even things that can bring physical suffering or destruction are not to be feared when they trust in You.

Help me remember that You appointed them to be born in such a time as this, and that You have prepared good works for them to do (Ephesians 2:10). In an era of dragons, You are raising up dragon slayers. May my children be mighty warriors in and for Your kingdom.

Section 1

SELFLESS PRAYERS FOR SELF

Craving for the Word

Lord Jesus, You *are* the Word of God. When I crave the Word, I crave You. I pray that You would give me an insatiable desire for the Word. I pray that when I am seeking guidance, You would turn my heart toward reading Your eternal truths.

I pray that when I miss my quiet time, You would give me discomfort, like when I'm hungry or thirsty. And when I feel like I can't retain information, please help me to remember Your words. When I'm going about my duties for the day, may Your words be present in my mind.

I pray that as I study, reading Your words would fill me with joy. Please bring others into my path who will study with me.

Oh God, Your Word is a lamp unto my feet and a light unto my path (Psalm 119:105). May every cell in my being crave the knowledge that comes from Your Word.

Eternal Perspective

God, I want to invest in what will last into eternity, but the temporary things of this world keep taking my attention. Please reshape my perspective and help me prioritize what matters most.

I pray for spiritual eyes to see the things that will have eternal weight, no matter how mundane they feel right now. Some battles are mine to fight while others are just distractions. Please give me the wisdom to tell the difference between the things that are my responsibility and the things that are not. Even if they are good, they may not be "mine" to carry. May I be faithful to what You have given me, knowing that the fruits of my obedience will last after I am gone. I praise You that I have more than just this life to live for. Help me to live it well, knowing that faithfulness in even the smallest of callings will echo long into eternity.

Wise Use of Money

Lord, You say so much about money in the Bible because You know how big of a stronghold money issues can become. I do not want You to ever have to compete for my heart. Keep my security in You, not in our bank account.

Everything that is done in secret will be brought to light (Luke 8:17), so I pray that our family will manage our resources in a manner that's above reproach. I pray for holy conviction regarding how our family makes money. May we bring a ministry mindset into whatever our hands find to do (1 Corinthians 10:31), conducting ourselves with integrity, even if it costs us financially.

Let how our family spends money be a conscious decision rather than an unguided habit. Prompt me to be a cheerful giver, investing wherever I see You working. May I regard both my time and resources as ways to support Your work here on earth.

Give Me a Moldable Heart

Lord God, I pray for a moldable heart that is receptive to Your leading, Your teaching, and Your loving rebuke. You say in Your Word that a broken and contrite heart You will not despise (Psalm 51:17). There is a lot I have control over, but my heart is not one of those things. Only You can change my heart, so I ask for a heart that can hear Your reproof. God, criticism is never fun, but when I hear it, I pray for the strength of character to evaluate if what is said about me is true. May I never discount good counsel just because of who says it.

Lord, I pray for a heart that is growing daily in delight for the things that please You. And I pray to be resensitized to the things that grieve You; if something is contemptible to You, let it also be repulsive to me. Lord, if I have grown complacent toward the sin in the world, the themes in my TV shows and movies, may You return to me a godly sense of shock and displeasure at unrighteousness. Help me surround myself with things that uplift truth, purity, goodness, and all that is excellent and praiseworthy.

I pray You would reveal to me when I am participating in anything that increases hardness or numbness in my heart. May I have the boldness to remove those influences from my life. God, with every breath, I place myself back in submission to You, seeking to walk in a way that brings glory to Your name. Guide the decisions I make each day. I pray against any kind of pride that would puff me up, and may I see myself humbly and with sober judgment (Romans 12:3). Grant me, God, a heart that responds willingly to the hands of the Potter.

Self-Discipline

God, a body at rest tends to stay at rest, and I confess that I have allowed inertia to set in. Before I can even pray for self-discipline, I must actually *want* self-discipline—so please orient my desires toward that which will discipline my heart, body, mind, and emotions. Help me stick to a schedule that will encourage healthy, daily rhythms, but also grant me the wisdom to know when to be flexible.

When it comes to food, I pray You would help me desire what is nourishing. I pray over my attempts at physical exercise, asking that You would make my body crave movement and fitness. May I be a good steward of this body entrusted to me. I cannot serve others if my body cannot handle the load. So, for the sake of Your kingdom, give me an enjoyment of exercise, but also the knowledge and faith (yes, faith!) to rest when needed.

I pray for self-control when it comes to social media. May I use it for the purpose of connecting with others and not for zoning out. When it comes to my brain, Lord, I pray that I would not shy away from a challenge. Give me a love of learning that I can model to my children, especially when it comes to understanding You more.

I pray over the gifts and talents You've given me, that I would cultivate them to the best of my ability. There is nothing I have that was not given to me by You, oh God. May I seek to be a faithful manager of these gifts so that, one day, I will be proud to stand before You as one who has proven faithful to the task. I long to hear Your voice say, "Well done, good and faithful servant! You have been faithful with a few things...Come and share your master's happiness!" (Matthew 25:23).

A Life of Balance and Discernment

Lord, the Christian life can feel like a balancing act. What is wise in one situation is foolish in another (Proverbs 26:4-5). So, God, I pray for the discernment to know how to respond wisely in every situation.

Show me when to speak and when to be silent. Where a hug and encouragement are needed, give me the heart of a nurturer. When a rebuke needs to be spoken, please show me how to phrase it graciously. When it comes to my children, help me to know when to build up and when to tear down (Ecclesiastes 3:3), when to encourage and when to correct.

Lord, it is easy to focus too much on the tasks You have given me at the expense of being still and listening to You. Show me when to step back and wait for You to slay the giant, and when to step forward in boldness to do what seems impossible.

I pray I would be diligent enough to invest in the strengths You have given me, yet humble and persevering enough to grow in the areas where I am weak.

There is "a time to search and a time to give up" (Ecclesiastes 3:6). I pray You would show me when it is time to release things that are lost.

In all I do, I pray You would guide me in discernment. Give me the fortitude to remain untainted by the world, but also the willingness to go into the dark places where Your light needs to be shone. In all things, God, make me a representative of You, being part of this world but not of it (1 John 2:16). I pray for balance in all things except radical love and radical obedience to Your commands, knowing that obedience to Christ *is* the path to the Father (John 14:4-6) and radical love invites others to join the journey.

Stewarding My Body Well

Lord, You say in Your Word that our bodies are Your temples (1 Corinthians 6:19). I confess I have not kept Your temple the way I should. A thousand things vie for my attention; eating well and exercising keep sliding to the bottom of my to-do list. But I pray for the diligence and self-control to steward this body to Your glory. I could ask for all the self-discipline in the world (and I ask for that too!), but I know that often You work by *developing* our character rather than granting it.

My motivation begins with my desires, so I ask, Lord, that You would change my desires. I pray that I would crave and delight in the food my body needs to be healthy. I pray that I would enjoy the process of exercising. I pray that I would crave habits that make me stronger.

Father, please broaden my idea of what health looks like so I don't force my body into a size or shape it wasn't meant to be. As I age, may I accept my body's natural changes without shame or comparison. I thank You,

Lord, for the laugh wrinkles, the stretch marks, and the gray hair, as they are evidence of joy and a life well lived (Proverbs 16:31).

God, I pray that I would see my stewardship of this body as another way to serve my family well. And for the areas over which I have no control—my genes, diseases, or chronic illness—I pray that I would rely on Your grace for the ability to do what You have called me to. May I never judge myself by what You have given to others. I thank You for this body, Lord, and all it can do. May I take the call to steward it well as seriously as I take every other calling in my life.

Prayer over Blind Spots

Lord, no matter how much I crane my neck, I'll never be able to see my own blind spots. But You are *El Roi*, the God who sees, so I ask You to use Your Spirit, Your Word, and the people You've placed around me to reveal the parts of myself I cannot see.

Whittle away the obstacles that hinder my fellowship with You and with others. Pull back the defense mechanisms I've constructed to protect myself. May the correction of Your Word bring me to perfect sight. May I also remember that Your voice does not condemn; Your kindness leads me to repentance (Romans 2:4).

May I never use my "personality profile" to excuse my blind spots. Please bring people into my life who see what I don't; help them graciously reveal it to me, and help me receive their words well. Lord, may it be said of me that I am a woman who receives correction.

Section 2

SPIRITUAL PROTECTION FOR THE HOME TURF

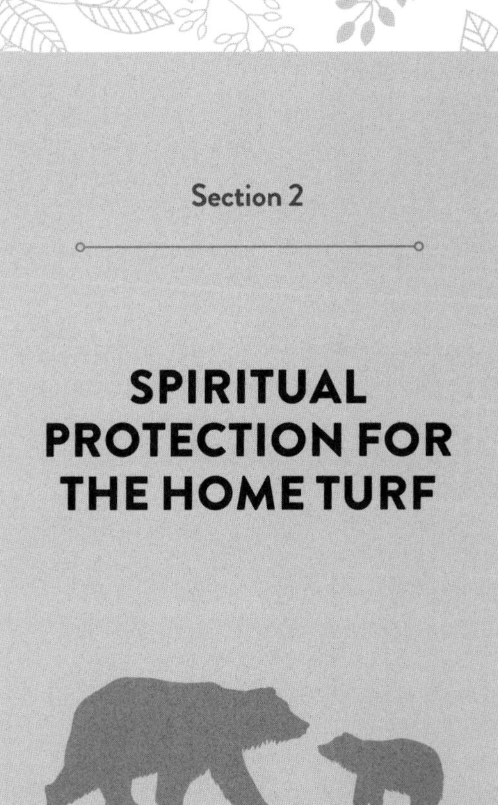

Bedroom

Lord God, I pray blessings over my bedroom, that it would be my sanctuary from the rest of the world, a place of refreshment and recharge.

Let this room be a place of intimacy between You and me, a space where I can confide to You my fears and my delights, mindful of how You provide for my needs. May this room be a bastion of prayer, my war room before I enter the world. As I shed my clothes each night, may I also shed the cares of the day and the sins of my heart. And as I get dressed in the morning, may I intentionally clothe myself in the armor of God (Ephesians 6:10-17).

Here in this place, increase my desires for You, Your Word, and Your presence. I praise You for all Your provisions and rejoice in the gentle kindness You show me morning by morning, evening by evening.

Kids' Bedrooms

Lord, I pray for this room, that it may be a sanctuary for [child]. I pray Your presence would permeate and rule over every square inch. I pray against any spirits of fear, loneliness, bitterness, lust, or [other struggles] that might try to influence [child].

I pray against any negative influences that would try to enter; may they be stalled at the door, unable to step foot inside. I pray against any spiritual "noise" that would prevent [child] from being able to hear Your voice here. May this room be a place where [child] can commune with You, [his/her] heavenly Father.

I pray that [child] would discover [his/her] gifts and strengths here. May this be a place for pondering Your truths, for exploring imagination and creativity. May this room be a fortress of calm in an often-chaotic world. Lord, spread Your hand of protection over this room. You are *Yahweh Shalom*, the God of peace.

Living Room

Lord, please protect and bless our living room, that it would be a place of family, friends, fun, and laughter. I pray against any spirits of discord, that this room would be a place of sweet fellowship.

I pray over the media that we consume in this room. Please convict us if (or when) we are watching something that will erode our desire for holiness. I pray for Your spirit of discernment to permeate this place. When the television depicts the world from an unbiblical perspective, help me and my kids to spot it and have fruitful discussion—separating good from bad, wise from unwise, truth from lies.

May this be a room of communion as we learn how to interact as a family and as hosts to guests. May the memories formed in this room be good, and may the lessons learned here be lasting. God, please come and be present here, today and every day.

The Digital Sphere

Lord, I pray for our family's use of the internet, screens, and social media. Please show us when giving [child] access to a device will be beneficial and when it will be harmful. We don't want to prevent the kind of learning that [his/her] peers are getting through interacting with technology, but neither do we want to impede [his/her] natural brain development by exposing [him/her] to more screen time than is healthy.

God, alert me to when [child's] physical or emotional health is being compromised by excessive use of technology. If or when that happens, may [his/her] father and I be willing to be the "bad guys" by taking it away. Please, God, let [child's] father and me be a united front. I pray for mutual agreement when it comes to our views about technology. Do not let any differences in perspective become a point of contention between us where [child] can play us against each other.

I pray for wisdom to know which apps to allow [child] to use and which to block. May we not bow to the whims of culture or popular opinion. Give us the words to articulate our reasons for not allowing [him/her] access so [he/she] doesn't think we are being arbitrary killjoys.

I pray that we adults would set a healthy example for responsible screen usage. May we never demand that our children be more disciplined than we are willing to be ourselves.

We thank You, God, for all the ways You bless us through technology. May we and our children know how to embrace the benefits without forming unhealthy addictions or habits.

Kitchen

Lord, I pray Your blessing over this kitchen. It is our constant reminder of our dependence on You as our daily bread.

I pray that the food we eat here would be chosen thoughtfully based on what *is* good, not just on what tastes good. (But Lord, let it be both!) We praise You for Your delicious gifts of fat and sugar; may we enjoy them in moderation. Lord, modify our taste buds to crave what nourishes our bodies, just as You shape our character to crave what is holy and pleasing.

As we prepare this meal, Lord, prepare our hearts. May we not resent the drudgery of the task but be thankful for what You have provided. Bless our time around the table; please make it a time of connection and not of contention. May the words we share grow our family bonds and honor You.

15

Grandparents' House

Lord, I thank You for the gift of extended family. Thank You that my children have living grandparents who love them. Abba Father, I pray over my [parents'/in-laws'] house as my children and I spend time here. Let the time we share here be full of love and laughter, as generations come together to impart and receive wisdom. I pray that my children would be oblivious to any area of contention between me and my [parents/in-laws], and that any old disagreements would be left at the door as we establish new relationships around this young generation.

Lord, I pray that Your wisdom would be spoken in this house. Please give my [parents/in-laws] the joy of investing in my children and pointing them toward You and Your truth. If there are areas of ideological disagreement between my [parents/in-laws] and us, I pray You would protect my children's minds from confusion. Then help us to address it with the kids later in a way that is fruitful and respectful of their grandparents.

I pray for grace as both my [parents/in-laws] and I are learning to navigate these new roles with new boundaries regarding grandchildren. Help me to walk in humility as a vessel of Your love to my [parents/in-laws], enjoying the days we have left with them. As far as it depends on us, may my husband and I model for our children a living example of what a healthy family should look like.

16

Child's Friend's House

Lord God, thank You for the gift of friends! I thank You that my child has relationships with other children, and I pray You would grow these friendships deeper and deeper. But God, I hear so many stories about things that happen at sleepovers or other visits to friends' houses. It makes me want to keep my children at home with me forever, but I know I can't do that.

So I pray special protection over [child] as [he/she] goes to [friend's] house. Grant [him/her] a special helping of discernment. If anything unhealthy is going on, I pray that [child] would be able to articulate it to me without feeling like a tattletale. If there are siblings in the home, I pray for protection against any kind of bullying, abuse, or inappropriate behavior. I pray You would give [child] the wherewithal to recognize if a situation is dangerous, the wisdom to remove [himself/herself] from it, and the boldness to speak if any boundaries were crossed. Protect [child's] mind when [he/she] is away from the safety of our nest.

And Lord, as [child] invites friends over to our house, help us provide a cocoon of safety against the world for all who enter. I pray that I would be the Mama Bear to each of [child's] friends—protecting, advocating for, and investing in them as they spend time in our home.

God, You did not give me a spirit of fear, but of love, power, and a sound mind (2 Timothy 1:7). I give You the fears I have when my child leaves the home and is outside of my protection. May I prepare [him/her] well enough to face challenges, remain steadfast, articulate the truth, and lead others into the beautiful knowledge of Your goodness.

Section 3

FROM BZZZZ!!! TO ZZZZZ...

Short Prayers for the Daily Grind

Upon Waking Up

Oh Lord, my God, Maker of heaven and earth, I praise You for another day of life. You alone know what today holds. May I work cheerfully and with contentment, taking joy in the tasks You have put before me. Give me energy when I'm tired, joy when I'm stressed, and the eyes to see what is most important for the day. I invite You, God, into my every moment. "May these words of my mouth and the meditation of my heart be pleasing in your sight, Lord, my Rock and my Redeemer" (Psalm 19:14).

Prayer from Head to Toes

Lord, I pray for [person/child/spouse] from [his/her] head to [his/ her] toes.

I pray over [his/her] feet; may [he/she] walk in ways pleasing to You—not departing to the left or the right (Proverbs 4:27).

I pray over [his/her] legs; may [he/she] have the strength to persevere through hardship.

I pray for [his/her] stomach; may [he/she] not be ruled by desires but by that which is pure, nourishing, beneficial, and life-giving.

I pray over [his/her] shoulders as [he/she] bears up under heavier burdens than [he/she] thinks [he/she] can hold.

I pray for [his/her] neck; may it not become stiff to Your reproach.

I pray for [his/her] head; may it be filled with light and truth, love and peace, and the knowledge of You.

Blessing over Quiet Time

Lord, I thank You for Your Word. I thank You that it is living and active, capable of molding my heart, mind, soul, and spirit (Hebrews 4:12). Please speak to me as I open these pages; instruct, correct, rebuke, encourage, equip, and give me hope. Even when the reading seems dry, remind me that I cannot leave Your Word unchanged. May every moment I spend in the Bible leave me with an insatiable longing for more. May I be equally motivated to not just know *about* You, but to actually know *You*.

Before the Tasks I Don't Enjoy

Lord, it's time for [task] again. I know I am to be thankful in all circumstances, so I thank You for [task] (1 Thessalonians 5:18). I know I am to do all things as unto the Lord, so may I never degrade any part of my job (Colossians 3:23). [Task] is no less glorifying to You than the larger or more enjoyable tasks. Help me rejoice in the smallness of these tasks, knowing my obedience is itself an act of worship. Oh God, I want to worship You in all things! So please, accept this small act of faithfulness as my way of singing Your praises. Reward me in this tiny act of submission by molding my character even more into the likeness of Your Son.

Preparing to Reengage with Kids

Lord, as I sit in the carpool line, use this time to refine me in the process of waiting. May I not be consumed by the unfinished things on my to-do list. Prepare me to interact well with my children as they climb in the car, excited or distressed about their day. May I show joy toward the things that excite them and compassion toward the things that have hurt them. Help me give them space if they need time to process their day silently. Alert me to anything unspoken on their hearts while still giving them the freedom to come to me in their own time, instead of forcing it out of them. When I have needs, may I clearly and gently verbalize them. I pray that You would attune each of us to the needs of the other as we embark on the next phase of the day at home.

Before Watching Entertainment

Lord, You are the author of beauty and laughter, and we praise You as the original artist. You are the great weaver of stories. As we sit down to enjoy this [show/movie/concert], may Your laws of goodness be ever before us. Sharpen our minds as we enjoy these gifts, so we may discern what is good and pleasing about this story and what is not. Where there are lies, please point them out. May we never grow desensitized to sin, and may we always crave the good things You have created.

Before Putting Kids to Bed

How can going to bed for one creature cause such misery when it's all *this* creature wants to do? Lord, please do not let tonight be another battle. I pray for patience when [child] keeps getting up. May I remember that I am the parent and [he/she] is the child. May I not give in to [child's] whims just because it is easier. May I be consistent with the little things so I need not wrestle as much with the big things. Please bless my child with a healthy exhaustion, and let each day end in sweet snuggles and sleepy kisses. And even when they don't, may I still count it all a blessing to be the mother of this child.

Release at the End of the Day

Another day has come and gone, full of things I can no longer change. You alone, Lord, know what was really accomplished today. For the areas of success, I thank You for Your goodness. I pray that anything sown through my sin would be forgotten and that I would learn from my mistakes. Let the things sown from Your power multiply, echoing into eternity. Where I have erred or hurt others, show me how to repent and make amends.

I release this day to You, in good and bad, in triumph and defeat. But no matter how today has gone, tomorrow is another day, every morning renewed with Your mercy (Lamentations 3:22-23 NASB). Give me refreshing sleep, Lord, and as I wake up, remind me once again that each day's battle belongs to You (1 Samuel 17:47).

Section 4

AGES, STAGES, AND RHYTHMS OF LIFE

To Not Screw Up My Toddler

Lord, You and [toddler] have something in common: Neither of you sleep! Give me meekness and patience with this little one. [Toddler] can't yet understand my words or my actions, so help me not to expect more of [toddler] than [he/she] is capable of. Tune my interactions to [his/her] frequency. Help me protect [him/her] when [he/she] can't even communicate [his/her] needs.

Free me from this fear that every mistake I make will become a fixture in my baby's psyche; it's just not true. When I reach my human limits, may I call upon Your strength. Please give me the wisdom and ability to know when I need to rest, and provide someone who can help me when I can't go on.

As I have forgotten the pain of childbirth, may my child forget all my mistakes as a learning mommy. Please hold up my arms when I cannot hold them up myself (Exodus 17:12).

Children Exploring Independence

Thank You so much for the immense honor and blessing of being the mama to these beautiful children. Lord, please make Your presence known to these sweet little ones. As they are in situations that require independence, Lord, gift them the confidence to step out from Mom and Dad while still looking back for guidance. Show me when to step in and when to step back and release them, allowing experience to be the better teacher for the lesson. May I never impede their learning when my protective instincts go on hyperdrive. Failure can be an irreplaceable teacher.

Lord, when my children's overconfidence puts them in an unsafe or unhealthy situation, please shelter them from any permanent harm. If I am distracted, may Your Spirit alert me to danger and prompt me to intervene. But most of all, help my children to understand the difference between defiance, rebellion, disobedience, and establishing God-honoring and developmentally appropriate independence.

For a Child with Separation Anxiety

God, help [child] to walk into school today without having to be carried like a surfboard. Give [child] the peace only You can bestow, reminding [him/her] that [he/she] is safe in Your arms and that You are always with [him/her].

Give me the patience and grace to reassure [child] when [he/she] is anxious. Help me understand where [his/her] fears are coming from and to offer [him/her] biblically rooted comfort so [he/she] knows why [he/she] can have confidence and peace.

Help me focus on what [he/she] needs and not on the opinions of onlookers as [child] transitions into the classroom today. I ask for wisdom to know when to guide [him/her] through these moments step-by-step and when to back away. Help me love this beautiful child made in your image like You do. Though I may fail [him/her] sometimes, I pray that [he/she] knows that You never will.

Blessing over Children on Their Birthdays

To be read over your child on his/her birthday

Oh God, we thank You for [child]. [Child], you are precious to us every day, but we especially celebrate you today.

We speak blessings over you, praying that you see yourself the way God sees you. We echo the delight He felt when He created you. May God bless you to know your true worth in Him so that your heart overflows with compassion, mercy, and love. We praise God for how He made you, knowing He decided in advance which gifts, skills, and interests would prepare you to fulfill His calling for your life. We rejoice as you discover who God created you to be. As you grow up in our home and beyond, may we always steer you toward God's heart and truth and then release you to His plans—the plans He had for you before you were ever born.

[Child], may God bless you to have wisdom in all situations, to know when to be a courageous warrior and when to be a compassionate healer. We pray for you to recognize truth and reject the enemy's lies. We are grateful you are a member of our family—a member who belongs, who is loved, and who will always have a home with us. We pray that you never crave the praise of others because you have known what it means to be fully accepted right here in this home and before God.

[Child], may the Lord bless you and keep you. May He be gracious to you and give you peace (Numbers 6:24-25). And may you use the blessings we speak over you this day to turn around and bless the world, making the name of Jesus beautiful in the eyes of those who do not know Him. Blessed be the name of the Lord for creating you, our precious [child].

School Decision

God, give our family the wisdom to make the right decision about the kids' schooling. I don't like what I hear about what's being taught in the schools. I don't like the behavior I am seeing tolerated, and I don't like the values being promoted. Oh God, please guide us.

If homeschool is where You are leading us, let me remember that You don't call the equipped; You equip the called. Provide me with a community of like-minded Mama Bears who are serious about preparing children for the world, not sheltering them from it.

Lord, if a Christian school will make the difference in my child's well-being, then I pray You would show our family what we need to do to make it happen. May we not use Christian schooling as a crutch or an excuse to disengage from our roles as spiritual leaders, but rather see it as a resource to fortify what we're already teaching our kids.

If public school is our only option, then I'll need

Your help to prepare my child. I pray for the wisdom and empowerment to teach my children to interpret reality according to truth and not the spirit of the age. May You open my children's eyes to the lies of culture as I seize every learning opportunity to reinforce objective, biblical discernment.

Whatever sacrifices we need to make, I pray we would do so joyfully, knowing we are investing in something far greater. God, where resources are limited, provide where we are lacking.

Lord, I release any judgmental feelings I may have for the decisions other families make. Let us each steward our families according to Your direction and not in reaction to peer pressure or fear. Help us make the right decision each year for our children's schooling; may we choose what will best mold their character and prepare them for the future.

Pubescent Identity Crisis

Lord, have mercy; puberty is here. Please give me an extra dose of grace for [child's] unpredictability while not allowing bad attitudes to escalate and solidify. Help me delight not only in the child [he/she] was, but in the [man/woman] [he/she] is becoming.

God, I pray that I can roll with the chaos as [child] learns who [he/she] is. An athlete? An artist? A musician? Introvert? Extrovert? Help me give [child] the freedom to explore different parts of [his/her] personality and help me journey along with [him/her], not belittling the process even when I think it's dumb.

Don't let me sweat the small stuff, but please, please, Father, give me the wisdom to see when [child] is questioning the big stuff. Where sin or lies are tampering with [his/her] God-given identity, let me be ferociously protective. Give me wisdom to distinguish between harmless experimentation and harmful ideologies. Show me when to allow [child] to make mistakes and when to remove [him/her] from dangerous influences. Give me the willingness to face [him/her] when I need to step up as the parent instead of always trying to be [his/her] friend. Please surround me with godly community who will encourage me if or when I need to make tough decisions.

I pray for open communication with [child] as [he/she] decides which parts of [himself/herself] are open to interpretation, and which—as a follower of Jesus—are not. May the truth we have imparted to [child] from [his/her] youth carry [him/her] through these uncertain years of change and discovery. I pray You would show [him/her] Your faithfulness and goodness in all situations, so that [he/she] knows that [he/she] can always return to You, no matter how far [he/she] has strayed. And I pray that You would parent *me* as I try to parent [him/her] through this beautiful but difficult season.

Releasing My Almost-Adult Children

Heavenly Father, time flies, and now I find myself on the brink of launching my children into adulthood. I often long for the days of naps, never-ending snacks, and the certainty that my children were safely within the four walls of our home. Now as they drive solo down busy streets and tackle important decisions on their own, I often struggle with anxiety and fear. Have we done enough? Are my children prepared enough?

Oh God, I cry out to You for their safety and protection. Please help me navigate this new stage, holding on lightly and not too tightly, reminding me that they are Yours. Above all, I pray they will remain anchored in Your truth, Your love, and Your promises, growing closer to You each day. Lord, help me to release [children] to Your care, trusting in Your plans and purposes for their lives. And may You feather this soon-to-be empty nest with precious memories.

Adult Children to Walk Faithfully with God

Father, I did my best to raise my children up to know and love You. I've disciplined them when necessary, just as You have disciplined me. But I know they are now responsible for their own choices—and the consequences of those choices.

My adult children face the same temptations today as Adam and Eve faced in the garden: to take their eyes off You long enough to doubt Your love and goodness. I pray for moral strength as their flesh cries out to be satisfied by temporal enticements, that my children would have a deeper and more abiding love for You than they do for the world's distractions.

Father, please give my adult children a community of believers who will encourage them in their faith. Please surround them with mature believers who will hold them accountable to Your perfect law, and give them a demonstrable love for others in both word and deed.

Section 5

FROM CLAY TO VESSEL

Prayers for My Kids' Spiritual Formation

Child's Salvation

Father, I desire for [child] to grow up in the fear and admonition of You. I desperately want [him/her] in [his/her] Father's house at a young age—just as Jesus was. I pray You would save [child] as soon as [he/she] can recognize the need for a Savior; I pray [he/she] can walk with You all the days of [his/her] life. Transform [his/her] heart of stone into a heart of flesh.

Only Your Holy Spirit can accomplish this. I am not the author of [his/her] salvation story; You are. Help me to trust You. Forgive me when I try to bring about my child's salvation storyline by my own means. No catechism, Sunday school, or Bible memorization can save [him/her] without Your Holy Spirit. Help me trust Your timing as well, Lord. Even if You change [his/her] heart later in life, I thank You still for Your tremendous grace.

Save [child]. Living Word, inscribe [his/her] name in Your Book of Life.

Child to Develop Personal Faith

Father, I pray You will help [child] develop a personal faith relationship with You. Not a hand-me-down faith that [he/she] "puts on" just because we "gave it" to [him/her] through church attendance. May [he/she] clothe [himself/herself] in righteousness through a salvation experience that is true, genuine, and unique.

I pray for [child] to grow in spiritual wisdom and godly stature as [he/she] learns to study the Word for [himself/herself]. May [child] learn to seek and find You through prayer and have a will that is conformed to Yours. Wrap [child] in fellowship and accountability within a theologically sound and spiritually robust local church that is committed to love and service. And then, Lord, may that cycle repeat itself through future generations of our family.

Kids to Love the Word

Father in heaven, more than [child] desires [his/her] favorite toys and TV shows, more than friends and social media, more than the approval of others, more than anything else—create in [child] an insatiable desire to know You through Your Word.

May [he/she] study, memorize, and meditate on Your truths so that [he/she] is prepared to share it with others. Never let [child] assume in arrogance that [he/she] knows all there is to know about You or Scripture. Give [him/her] a thirst for learning and the humility to change [his/her] theology when it is in contradiction to Your Word.

Most of all, may [child's] character, behavior, and attitudes be transformed by Your Word. Let Your kindness, patience, joy, peace, truthfulness, and love overflow out of [him/her] as [he/she] abides in You, the true vine (John 15:1-8). May others around [him/her] experience Your loving-kindness through [him/her], and be drawn to Your Word as well.

For Children to Love the Church

Heavenly Father, thank You for the church. Despite its flaws and imperfections, I pray my child would trust Your plan for the church and always be committed to a local body of believers—a community committed to truth, love, and obedience to Your Word. May [he/she] crave the fellowship and encouragement that can only be found in a community dedicated to following You.

Please provide trustworthy shepherds in [child's] life who will point [him/her] to Christ. You alone are the perfect Shepherd, and You promise to guide all Your children through green pastures, beside quiet waters, and even in the valley of the shadow of death (Psalm 23:1-4). While many human leaders strive to follow Your example, I know that they often fail to shepherd others according to Your perfect ways. Please protect [child] from any leaders who would abuse their authority, whether intentionally or otherwise, and especially guard [child] from any spiritual leaders who are misusing Your Word for their own ends.

Give [child] wisdom and discernment as [he/she] participates in the church's mission. Help [him/her] to vigilantly protect their church body with sound doctrine, and give [him/her] eyes to recognize when compromise or coldness is sneaking in. May [he/she] stand against the wicked schemes of those who would attack Your church, whether from inside or outside the walls (Acts 20:29-30).

Help [child] to find friendship and fellowship as [he/she] discovers which gifts You have given [him/her] for the edification and building up of the church (1 Corinthians 14:12). Guide [child] to love and support the people and the ministries of [his/her] local church through prayer, deeds, and words of affirmation. Allow [him/her] to have healthy experiences in church that reveal the beauty of the gospel message and encourage [him/her] to stay rooted in a faith community for a lifetime.

Fostering Gratitude and Contentment

Lord, I pray for godly contentment in [child]—a virtue that can only come through gratitude. It is so hard when [his/her] friends are getting things we cannot afford. My child may not have the best of everything, but [he/she] has everything needed for life, godliness, and good works (2 Peter 1:3; 2 Corinthians 9:8). I pray that [he/she] would not compare [his/her] own situation against [his/her] peers or covet that which is not [his/hers].

Bring it to [child's] attention when others have *less* than [he/she] does; may [he/she] see it as an opportunity to practice generosity. I pray You would give [him/her] the eyes to see the non-tangible gifts You have provided: a loving family, safety, security, and a peaceful home with parents who love [him/her]. Not every child can say the same. May [he/she] value what You value and only yearn for that which will aid in advancing Your kingdom.

Healthy Outlets for Emotions

Lord, being a kid is hard. Little people can have big emotions and lots of them. Help me to be patient as I teach [child] to identify [his/her] emotions and then choose healthy outlets to express them. Our culture platforms and applauds people who spew their every feeling, equating emotional outbursts with "speaking truth." I pray that [child] would feel comfortable expressing [his/her] feelings without erupting into emotional rants.

Help me coach [child] to identify what emotion [he/she] is feeling and why so that [he/she] can respond appropriately and productively. I pray I would help [child] channel [his/her] emotions in a healthy way, reminding [him/her] that the best art, the most beautiful songs, and the fiercest athletes are often the result of passions directed toward constructive ends.

Give me the eyes to see when [his/her] behaviors are hiding big feelings that [he/she] doesn't know how to express. I pray especially over frustration, as this one emotion can be the root cause of many behavioral issues.

As [child] learns to identify [his/her] emotions, may [he/she] use this knowledge to develop healthier coping mechanisms. I pray that this introspection would not lead to self-preoccupation, but rather to a greater sense of self-control and the ability to empathize with others.

Lord, I say all this as I look in the mirror. I can sometimes let my own emotions get overrun by my child's emotions, and then I find myself modeling all the things I'm trying to teach [child] *not* to do. Please grant me grace and levelheadedness to be the example I want [him/her] to follow.

When Kid Makes a Big Mistake

Oh Lord, [child] has made a mistake and doesn't know what to do about it. May this be the beginning of [child] getting to know You as the one who can restore all things. Help [child] to recognize and admit where [he/she] has failed, and then own up to the consequences. Use this uncomfortable lesson for [child's] sanctification.

Help me teach [child] to approach Your throne with confidence and without fear, so that [he/she] may receive mercy for [his/her] failures (Hebrews 4:16). And may [child] know me as a safe place where [he/she] can confess [his/her] mistakes instead of hiding them, even when [he's/she's] messed up big-time.

As I help [child] deal with the fallout, may I reflect Your grace and forgiveness while encouraging [him/her] to reach out to make amends and right whatever damage [his/her] actions may have caused. Thank You, God, that You can use even our failures for Your glory.

Discerning God's Voice from Other Voices

Oh Lord, the world can be so loud, and sometimes deafening. [Child] is bombarded with so much information, much of it distorted by lies. Getting distracted from the truth of Your Word is so easy amid today's clamor and chaos.

God, help [child] to discern the difference between Your voice and the voices of those influenced by the world. Keep [child] mindful of the deceiver's tactics, and constantly remind [him/her] to test every message [he/she] hears against the truths of Scripture, reason, and reality. Help [him/her] know that the battle for discernment isn't always between overt good and evil, but as Charles Spurgeon said, "between right and almost right."

Lord, the enemy wraps his most potent lies in partial truths. Protect my child from believing deadly deceptions that sound good, loving, and even Christlike. Keep [child's] heart tuned in to Your voice, knowing that You are always at work even when You seem silent.

For Child's Sin to Be Exposed

God, no beating around the bush here: If [child] is sinning, please expose it. If [he/she] is heading down a dangerous road, please let [him/her] get caught—like, *every time*. Please provide people around [child] who are bold enough to tell me if they see problematic behavior. I pray for keen Mama Bear instincts that would alert me to sin-in-the-camp before the behavior gets out of control. I pray that [child's] conscience would kick into overdrive, and that [he/she] would exhibit unmistakable, telltale signs of a guilty conscience when [he/she] knows [he/she] is doing wrong.

Most of all, I pray that the outcome of being caught would be [child's] correction and restoration. I pray that I would faithfully correct this behavior while [child] is still under my charge so that future authorities do not have to do the job I should have already done. Please show me how to pick my battles, and may I never turn a blind eye to sin because I'm too tired to deal with it.

When discipline is needed, I pray that You would give me the insight to know which punishment will be the most effective for this particular child. When there are natural consequences for [his/her] actions, may I resist the impulse to swoop in and protect [him/her] (Ecclesiastes 8:11). Most of all, may [child] develop [his/her] own moral conscience so that [he/she] doesn't need to be caught in order to repent.

Reconciliation and Forgiveness When Hurt

Father, I pray for [child] as [he/she] is having trouble forgiving [person]. Please help [child] to come to terms with the pain so that [he/she] can begin moving on in a healthy way. May [he/she] first examine [himself/herself] honestly and see where [he/she] has any fault in the matter. I pray that healthy conviction—not shame-filled condemnation—would cause [him/her] to repent, seek forgiveness, and also to forgive [himself/herself].

Let [child] do what [he/she] can to seek peace over this issue with [person]. Help [child] to see that [he/she] can only be responsible for [himself/herself] and not [person's] reaction. If it's Your will, Lord, we pray for reconciliation between [child] and [person].

Give [child] the ability to release this hurt and to move forward. Help [him/her] set appropriate boundaries while still extending grace and mercy. As far as it depends on [him/her], let [child] live at peace with others (Romans 12:18).

Cultivating Sexual Faithfulness

Heavenly Father, my precious child is coming of age in a time when puberty and sexuality have never been more confusing. I feel woefully unprepared for the things [child] will have to face. Please direct me to resources that will help me explain the goodness of Your design. Soften my heart and open my ears when [he/she] comes to me with questions, so I can first listen and understand before jumping to a response. Show me where I need to initiate conversations and when to allow my children to come to me. I pray that I become the safest place for [child's] questions so that [he/she] does not feel the need to ask friends or Dr. Google.

God, help [child] to move beyond the simplistic concept of abstinence and toward a more holistic understanding of healthy and holy sexuality—how it reflects and informs [his/her] entire worldview and even [his/her] perception of You! Guide [child] as [he/she] thinks about the kind of person [he/she] would like to marry. I pray that [child] would want to save sex for marriage out of a desire to honor You, honor [himself/herself], honor [his/her] future spouse (Romans 1:24), and protect [his/her] future marriage. I pray that You would place godly leaders around [him/her] who will reinforce these concepts so it's not just coming from [his/her] stuffy, old parents. And especially, Lord, give [him/her] friends committed to the same sexual values.

Holy Father, please protect [child's] eyes and mind from pornography so that [his/her] understanding of sex is not tainted with vulgarity, degradation, and violence. Please convict [him/her] when [he/she] is watching television or movies with graphic sexual content. Help [him/her] understand that what is on the screen can warp [his/her] idea of what sex will be like one day. May all [his/her] decisions be in preparation for a healthy and fulfilling sex life in [his/her] future marriage.

Section 6

THINGS MY KIDS HAVE TO DEAL WITH

Stewarding Popularity Well

Lord, I thank You for the favor You have granted [him/her] in the eyes of others. Whatever Your purpose is for this, I pray [he/she] will always recognize that with popularity comes a responsibility to represent You well. Please guard [him/her] from being puffed up or from looking down on others. Help [him/her] handle this mantle with grace and goodness, using [his/her] influence to show compassion and kindness to those seen as outcasts.

Whatever influence You grant [child], may [he/she] use it to bring about good for others and Your kingdom. And if this is a season that passes from [him/her], may [child] adjust to the change without growing bitter or trying to regain "the glory days." Keep [him/her] from growing addicted to positive attention. There will be a day when [he/she] needs to stand up for truth in an unpopular way, and on that day, may [he/she] seek Your approval alone.

Dealing with Rejection

Lord, rejection cuts right to our very core, telling us we are unworthy and unwanted. I pray that [child] would be able to receive the truth: that You created [him/her] with beautiful and ultimate worth, and that no human opinion can change that. Fill [child] with Your peace, Your confidence, Your strength, and Your love.

Lord, we praise You for allowing us to feel rejection, as You, too, were rejected and despised by men (Isaiah 53:3). Please use this painful experience to foster intimacy with [child], and enable [him/her] to flip this rejection on its head—that it would not result in defeat but in empowerment, spurring [child] to speak hope and life into other kids who feel crushed under the weight of rejection. Lord, I pray that [he/she] may be able to show others their value and worth, pointing them to You as their Lord and Savior as well.

When My Child Feels Alone in Following Christ

Lord, please be near [child] when [he/she] stands alone as the only one of [his/her] peers truly seeking to follow You and live according to Your commands. In [his/her] school, [his/her] job, or even in the youth group—Lord, be [child's] support system when [he/she] feels alone.

When rejected, remind [him/her] that the world hated You first (John 15:18). I pray You will take [his/her] shame and one day replace it with praise and renown (Zephaniah 3:19). Comfort [child] when [he/she] is fearful of retribution for being faithful to Your Word, and give [him/her] courage to endure any consequences for standing firm in Your truth. Give [child] a healthy self-respect that allows [him/her] to act upon [his/her] convictions while exercising Your kindness that leads to repentance (Romans 2:4).

Protect [child's] heart and mind from lies of the enemy, especially if the enemy tries to convince [him/her] that living for You is not worth the cost. May [he/

she] count it all joy that the testing of [his/her] faith is worth the spiritual maturity as You make [him/her] perfect and complete (James 1:2-4). And as [child] develops a wholehearted devotion to You, may it never come at the expense of loving like Jesus loved. As [he/she] walks according to Your commands, may [he/she] be the hands and feet of Jesus to those who reject [him/her], developing a healthy humility and not succumbing to self-righteous comparison.

Good Friends for My Son

God, I pray for good friends for my son. I pray You would provide him with other boys who share his interests and have a desire to pursue You. I pray for laughter and fun and plenty of scraped knees to go around. But I also pray for a friend who is aware enough to speak up before the group does something truly stupid and dangerous. When there is temptation to impress others, I pray they would exercise the wisdom, discretion, and common sense that are all too uncommon among a group of boys trying to outdo each other.

I pray against the temptation that boredom can bring. When trouble goes looking for them, may they be willing to turn the other way. I pray You would form in them a sense of godly bravery and independence. At the same time, when they are tempted to see how close to the fire they can get without being burned, I ask that Lady Wisdom would intervene before damage is done (Proverbs 8).

I pray for friends who will stand against a culture that tells them manhood is earned by using and disrespecting women. I pray that my son and his friends would be godly influences among the other boys at school, ready to protect *every* girl in their community—not just the ones they are interested in. May they stand against any dishonor or shame directed at others by their peers.

Grant my son friends who are ambitious enough to move beyond video games and into activities that cultivate their minds and bodies. I pray for emotional safety among them, so they are willing to say the hard things to each other when one of them steps out of line. Above all, may they spur one another on toward godliness and good deeds, and may these boys grow into men of honor (Hebrews 10:24).

Good Friends for My Daughter

Friendship is so good, Lord! But it's not always easy to find or make friends. My heart aches for [daughter] to find deep, lasting friendships—or at the very least, good friends for this season.

Please help my daughter to make friends. Give her the kind of friend who will text her to meet at the park or just to chat, a friend who will share a lunch when she forgets hers, or a friend who will wait for her on the swings. She needs a friend with whom she can share her secrets, and someone to turn to for advice in a tricky situation. Please give her friends who not only have kindness and humor, but also discernment and conviction.

Lord, please give her these kinds of friends, and help her to become a good friend too; lead her to become kind, gentle, loyal, and wise. And as these friends grow up and face more challenges, may these relationships serve to sharpen each girl. May they point each other toward Christ and away from the ways of the world.

I pray for a friend who has [daughter's] back when

other girls seek to tear her down. Please make them brave together as they stand against peer pressure and the temptation to compromise. I pray that the security they find in each other will protect them from trying to get unhealthy attention from boys; may they hold one another to a higher standard than this culture demands. I pray they would say hard things to each other, pray together, study together, and praise You together.

I pray for bonds that will last a lifetime. And even if she cannot yet build this kind of epic, lifelong friendship, please allow my daughter to have just enough good-hearted friends this year to not feel lonely. Thank You, Lord, for friendship, and for hearing my prayer.

Nightmares

Oh Lord, my poor [child] keeps having nightmares. They disturb me, too, and my sleep. You are the light, Lord; nothing is hidden from You, so I am asking You to bring the source of these bad dreams to light. If [child] is filling [his/her] mind with dark images, may these dreams serve to remind [him/her] how important it is to guard our eyes.

As [his/her] mom, give me compassion to help [child] through this tough night. In Your great mercy, I call on You to restore sweet slumber to my child. Show [child] that [his/her] nightmares are not real, but Your comfort is; Your Word is the lullaby to our souls, because "greater is He who is in you than he who is in the world" (1 John 4:4 NASB). May we both be able to lie down and sleep in peace, oh Lord, for You make us dwell in safety (Psalm 4:8).

Dating

Oh God, here we go. How did we get here so fast? Honestly, I have dreaded this moment because I know all the things that can go wrong—the hurt, the temptation, the danger, and the pressure. I pray that [child] would discover what [he/she] needs and wants in a future spouse without picking up baggage from dating that will make [his/her] marriage more difficult. I pray [he/she] and whomever [he/she] dates would get to know one another without placing themselves in positions that will tempt them to behave like husband and wife rather than boyfriend and girlfriend; give them wisdom to set healthy, godly boundaries and the internal motivation to stick to them.

May [child] treat each significant other in the way [he/she] hopes [his/her] future spouse is being treated. For every relationship that does not end in marriage, I pray that the two would be able to part on friendly terms, both able to say without hesitation that they prepared the other to be an even better husband or wife for someone else, and also able to speak well of each other.

Keep [his/her] father and me attuned to any red flags or danger signs as [child] navigates this new realm. Heaven forbid that [he/she] be harmed in any way in this relationship, but if so, show me how to handle it in a way that still honors You while advocating for [child]. Be the mender of [his/her] heart if or when it is broken. Protect [his/her] ability to trust others in the future, knowing that if nothing else, [he/she] will always be able to trust You. God, I wish we could just fast-forward to marriage, but I know that's not how this works. I pray that any negativity I might have from past bad dating experiences would not hinder my ability to help [child] navigate the world of dating.

Teenagers with Raging Hormones

Father, please help me love my crazy teenagers. Help me to endure every sarcastic remark and angry rebuttal uttered in a hormonal haze. Help me love them through every eye roll, grunt, and exasperated sigh. Remind them they really do want to learn about their changing bodies from their father and me and not from the world. Even when they act embarrassed of our love, remind me that they secretly appreciate the tenderness and care.

Please protect our relationships—I remember the friction between me and my own mother, and I do not want this for me and my kids. Help me to teach my children to honor You with their actions and speech even when they feel completely off-kilter. May our home not be ruled by their constantly changing emotions. Help me to be empathetic to their struggles without enabling an improper response.

Help me remember that this stage will eventually pass, and in place of my bright children will be bright young adults. And be with my kids' father and me as we navigate this new stage of development. Remind us what it felt like at that age so we can be gracious yet firm for the good of our teenagers' spiritual development. This situation is not unique to us or to our children. You created their bodies and hearts to endure these changes. Please help us to coexist peacefully together. Though our home is hormonal, may it still be a happy one.

Pressure to Fit In

Lord, as [child] tries to decide who [he/she] is, I pray [he/she] will never lose a grip on biblical values. As [he/she] asks, "Who will I follow—the Lord or the world?" help [him/her] remember that Jesus Himself is the Way. Give [him/her] the heart and courage to take the narrow path that leads to righteousness; help [him/her] not be afraid to travel Your path alone until You provide friends to travel alongside [him/her].

May [child] embrace the adventure of following You in a culture that doesn't. Help [him/her] to speak with spiritual conviction unburdened by the condemnation of others. Use [his/her] strength under pressure to inspire [his/her] friends to desire You for themselves.

When the pressure feels like too much for [child] to bear, let our home be a release valve and let me be a refuge, encouraging [him/her] to use this pressure to become more like You and less like the world.

Protection Against Comparison

Lord, help me set reasonable expectations for myself and my children. When it comes to grades, sports, performance, friends, other moms, and other families, keep our eyes on You instead of on the standards set by others. Help us remember that our self-image is built on being made in the *imago dei*—image of God—not the *imago me*. Instruct me to know when average is okay. When failure happens—my own or my kids'—grant us humility to learn, improve, move on, and not be defined by it but rather *refined* through it. The jealousy monster is real. Let it not cause havoc in our house; may we slay it with the sword of Your Spirit, which is the Word of God.

Broken Hearts

God, [child] is hurting so badly right now. I pray that I would not minimize [his/her] heartache but would be a safe place for [him/her] to grieve, be vulnerable, and process these emotions.

Please meet my child in [his/her] sorrow, reminding [him/her] that there is no earthly pain You did not experience first. You were mocked. You were betrayed. You were rejected by Your best friends. Oh Lord, You say in Psalm 34:18 that You are close to the brokenhearted and save those who are crushed in spirit. Remind [child] of this promise.

God, I pray that [child] would feel this pain without being consumed by it. Help me give [him/her] the space to heal without giving [him/her] so much space that the pain spirals out of control. Give me the wisdom to know when to engage and when to back away. [Child] is Your child first and foremost. Please be with [him/her] while [his/her] heart is breaking.

Section 7

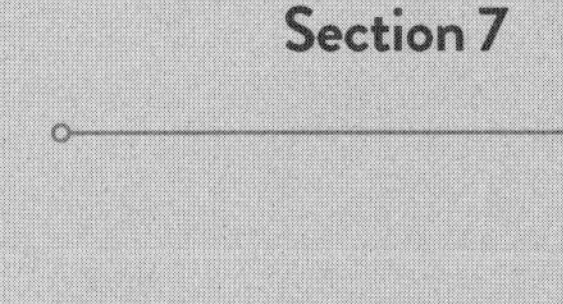

WELCOME TO THE RUMBLLLLLLE

When I Have Been Wronged (and Want to Release the Kraken)

Lord, I have been wronged and I am angry. I want You to bring down the fire and destroy those who have hurt me, but I know that's not how You work. I thank You that I can bring my pain, hurt, and desire for revenge and lay it at Your feet.

Please calm my heart as my brain replays the scene, reminding me of how "right" I was and how wrong [person] was. This kind of obsessing will not lead to Your righteousness. Instead, please show me how I have contributed to the situation. Even if I'm 99 percent right, I should still own the 1 percent where I'm wrong. But let's be honest...I'm probably not 99 percent guiltless.

Remind me of the times when I have been the one who has brought hurt. If I'm honest with myself, there is nothing that [person] has done to me that I haven't done to You first. Seventy times seven, times infinity, You have forgiven me. Who am I to withhold Your forgiveness from another?

Show me how to proceed in this situation and how

to wisely express my anger and hurt in a way that might lead to reconciliation. If returning to this relationship is unwise, please give me the strength to release [person] to You, knowing there is only so much I can do to establish peace.

God, forgiveness doesn't mean that what was done is suddenly okay. Forgiveness is exempting myself from being judge and jury. Give me Your power to take the high road, even when I want so badly to grab justice for myself. You say vengeance is Yours to repay (Deuteronomy 32:35). Bring to light what needs to be brought to light. Give me the patience to wait for You to right the wrongs done to me—in Your time and in Your way.

Before Engaging in Conflict Resolution

Lord, as I approach this conflict zone, I pray for humility to see my own flaws, grace to see where others are hurting, patience to navigate defense mechanisms, and strength to absorb whatever anger is sent in my direction. Make me an instrument of Your peace, remembering that the path to peace is sometimes painful. Sweeping things under the rug does not lead to resolution. Give me the courage to bring unpleasant things into the open. May we work toward *actual* peace, not just the appearance of it.

Help me release any blame unfairly placed on my shoulders and own any that is mine to own. Help me to repent without making excuses, and to grant mercy as I would want mercy granted to me. Above all, help me to see [person] through Your eyes of love as a fellow broken vessel still in the process of conforming to Your image.

Loving the Unlovable

Lord, I did not treat [person] the way I should have. I recognize how many times I've been unlovable, difficult, and socially awkward, yet You have loved me anyway. Thank You for never giving up on me.

God, I want to give mercy as I have received mercy (Matthew 5:7), and I need mercy so often. Make me an instrument of Your love and mercy and unconditional acceptance. Please bring to my attention when others overlook my flaws and oddities, so I in turn can do the same when others have flaws and oddities that annoy me. Help me take responsibility for the unloving way in which I treated [person], apologize sincerely, and do whatever else is needed to make amends. And tomorrow, give me a special helping of grace for [person], so I can love [him/her] with the compassion You have showered upon me.

58

When Everyone Is at Each Other's Throat

Lord, we stop right this moment to remember that we are not each other's enemies; we are on the same team.

God, we resist whatever spirits of confusion, anger, or miscommunication are trying to steal our joy. Once again we confess to being short-tempered, entitled, or quarrelsome. We humbly ask that You reveal to us individually where we have been wrong, and we pray You will guide us as we seek to heal whatever wounds were just created. I pray You would open our eyes to any pain the other is experiencing, so we might see each other with Your grace and compassion.

May Your spirit of peace enter this house and silence the voice of the accuser. We ask that clear communication and love be present in all our conversations. Lord, hem us in, "behind and before" (Psalm 139:5). Protect this home from anything that is causing strife and division.

Parenting the Children I Have (and Releasing Who I Think They Should Be)

Oh Lord, I couldn't wait to become a mom. I'll admit, I romanticized motherhood and created an idealized version of the child I expected to have. I imagined [his/her] life and future in ways that pleased my human heart. I pictured the sports [he/she] would play, the interests we'd share, the matching clothes we'd wear. But real life has shown me how my idealized vision of [child] is preventing me from loving the child I have. I confess that I often struggle to understand [him/her]. I am trying to parent [him/her] the way [he/she] needs to be parented, but I don't even know what [he/she] needs half the time—and when I try something that would have worked with me, it backfires. Sometimes, I just don't understand [him/her], and I know [he/she] doesn't understand me.

God, I pray You would open my eyes to areas where I am projecting my own expectations onto [child].

Please reveal to me the unique way You have made [him/her], that I may cultivate [his/her] strengths without fixating on [his/her] weaknesses. Help me to support [him/her] in the interests *You* have given [him/her], no matter how little they interest me. Lord, I don't want to stand in the way of [him/her] fulfilling *Your* plans for [him/her]. [Child] is Your child first.

Grant me a kingdom mindset and eternal vision for the child you have given me. Give me the courage to help mold [child] into *Your* image instead of trying to conform [him/her] to mine. As I mother [him/her], empower me to disciple [him/her] well according to the way You made [him/her].

Calming Down Before Disciplining My Child

Lord, I'm about to blow it—please hold me back! Calm me down. I feel so mad and need a time-out before I can lovingly dispense discipline, because right now it would not be coming out of love.

Give me compassion for [child] as You have shown me compassion time and time again. Let my motives be to restore and instruct [child], not to belittle [him/her]. Give me wisdom to make the punishment fit the crime, no more and no less.

You alone know what [child] needs to learn from this lesson. I release my anger to You. I thank You for the times when You have redirected me. Discipline is hard, but it produces a fruit of righteousness and peace for those who allow it (Hebrews 12:11). May everything I do be for my child's loving correction, so [he/she] will gain the skills to become a successful adult who loves and fears Your commands.

Asking for My Child's Forgiveness

Heavenly Father, I have blown it. More times than I care to mention, but especially right now. Today, I need to ask my child for forgiveness. Seeing myself more clearly has shown me how easily my sin can leave lasting scars on this little person You've given me to raise. Oh Lord, please protect my child's heart and mind from me when I fail to live as a loving example of Christ.

I thank Your Holy Spirit for pricking my pride and bursting my bubble of self-righteousness. I want to be a superhero mom, never making mistakes or messing up my witness in front of my kids. Yet here we are. I'm not a superhero. Today, I was the villain. As much as it humbles me to admit my error, isn't that Your point? I need to demonstrate humility that leads to repentance, and then form the words and get them out of my dry mouth.

Help me make my apology true—not sugarcoated, not euphemistic, and especially not in the form of an excuse. Help me to name exactly what I did wrong and why I need to ask for forgiveness. Lord, my children will learn how to repent and apologize based on how their father and I model these things. Use this apology as a demonstration that gives them the courage and permission to do the same whenever they have wronged another. Use it for my sanctification and for theirs.

Grant me patience if they are not able to forgive me right away. Help me release my disappointment in myself, knowing I have done what I can do to seek reconciliation. Please restore our relationship. And if my child has not yet accepted Your forgiveness for [his/her] sins, use this exchange to move [him/her] ever closer to You.

When I Really Don't Like Someone but Want To

Lord, I don't know if I can—or should—admit this out loud, so let's keep this between us: I am really struggling to like [person].

God, I thank You for the gift of relationships. I thank You for the value they serve in refining us and challenging us to live in community despite personality differences. I *want* to like [person]. I do. I know I cannot control anything but my own response, so I bring this to Your feet.

Lord, I pray for the ability to see [person] through Your eyes. I pray the things that bug me will just not bug me anymore—or at least will bug me less! You made [person]. You know [his/her] history, quirks, trauma, and triumphs. I know that when You think of [person], You can see a masterpiece where I just see a hot mess. I just don't see [person] the way You do, but I want to.

Remind me to speak encouragement when I see [person] doing whatever [he/she] does well. In the areas where we have personality differences, reveal to me the benefits of being like [person]. Where there is pain and [person] is acting out of fear or instinct, give me the words and actions to be a safe place. Where I feel misunderstood, please give me ability to communicate.

Lord, You say that as far as it depends on us, we are to live at peace with all people (Romans 12:18). So as far as it depends on me in this relationship, may I do and say the things that foster kindness, friendship, and closeness. Where things are outside of my control, I pray for the ability to release and to absorb—as You absorbed on our behalf.

63

Establishing Boundaries with Toxic Family Members

God, for the protection of those You have put in my care, I cannot subject my family to [person] anymore. Separation from others is never Your first plan, but I've done everything I can possibly do to live with [person] in a peaceful relationship, and it is no longer healthy.

[Person] is family, and I cannot just cease all relationship, so please give me Your wisdom to place firm and healthy boundaries for the good of our family, God. I pray for our hearts as we heal from this broken relationship. I pray You would give us eyes to see where You are working in [person's] life, and may we also celebrate each victory together. But where there is recalcitrance and hardness, God, may our hearts not become wounded and calloused.

Lord, living at peace with everyone does not always mean subjecting ourselves to their presence. We can live at peace from a distance, knowing You are the restorer of all things. God, please work in [person's] heart, showing [him/her] how [his/her] actions are pushing people away. I know [he/she] does not want to be alone, and I know that a person would never act in the way [person] does unless they were in a lot of pain. So, Lord, bring healing to the parts of [him/her] that need it. I pray that I would communicate our family's need to separate in a way that is unemotional and leaves the door open for future relationship should [person's] behavior change.

God, I know it is only by Your grace that I have not found myself in the same situation as [person]. Please search my heart for the areas where I have wounded others. May I never be at rest with my own sin. Thank You for bringing all things to light and restoring all things in eternity.

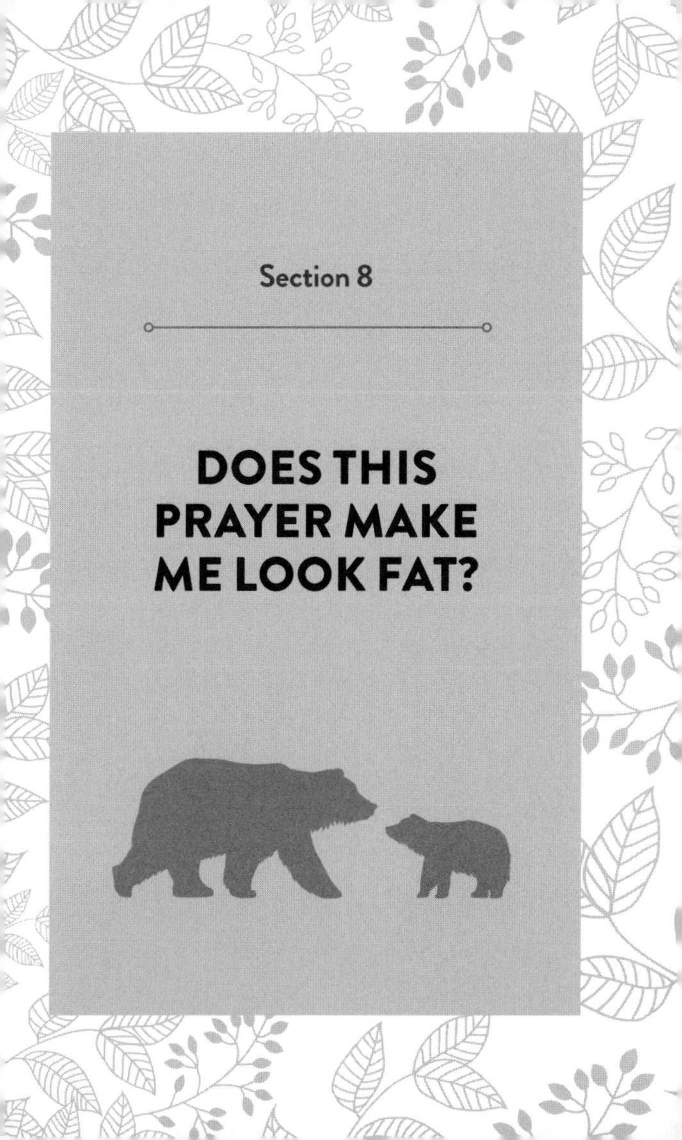

Section 8

DOES THIS PRAYER MAKE ME LOOK FAT?

When I Just Want to Pee Alone

Dear God, I'm so grateful for my children, but some days I just want to pee alone. I miss my life before them. I miss *me* before them. I miss sleeping peacefully, cooking whatever I wanted, leaving the house whenever I wanted, and going wherever I wanted. Is that too much to wish for? Good grief, nothing humbles you like motherhood.

Thank You, God, for the reminder that it's not all about me. Help me to remember how sacred this calling is. Help me to cherish my children and serve them sacrificially without expecting appreciation or reciprocation. Help me remember that this is a special season. Before long I will have "me" back, and then I will miss these days with *them*. Help me to remain grateful, patient, and loving. But in the meantime, I feel like I could really regroup if I could, just this once, pee without an audience.

When Social Media Has Warped My View of Motherhood

Lord, thank You for the blessings that social media can bring. Motherhood can be so isolating, and sometimes the virtual community can feel like the only community I have. However, I pray You would help me realize when I'm using social media because I have a desire to escape instead of a desire to connect.

I confess, Lord, that I often interact more with people online than I do the people in my own church. This isn't healthy; it prevents me from seeking in-person fellowship. I fixate on an edited version of myself and others instead of focusing on real life. And I believe the lies social media promotes about what motherhood should look like.

Please forgive me for the times I've allowed pictures to shape my parenting more than Your Word. I judge myself for not taking the vacations, making the crafts, or creating the experiences that other mothers provide. I curate my profile trying to deceive others into thinking my family has the picture-perfect life; meanwhile,

I participate in other moms' likewise deception toward me. We fight and inwardly compete over who has crafted the best façade, holding ourselves to a standard that we all know isn't real. Why do we do this to ourselves? Oh God, why am I allowing it to continue?

Human approval, praise, likes, and comments have fueled this addiction, and I repent of making my vanity a higher priority than authenticity, humility, and the discipleship of my child. In my desire to be perfect in ways that don't matter, I've missed opportunities to demonstrate Your love and grace in ways that do. Give me the strength to break off any addictions to social media that are fueling the problem. Change my desires. Change my values. May I fear losing out on Your refining fire more than I fear losing out on meaningless online engagement.

When My Mouth Gets Me in Trouble

Oh Lord, You say in Your Word that the tongue is the hardest member of the body to control. I did not honor You in my speech today. I pray for the humility to apologize to those I have hurt. I cannot say I didn't mean what I said, because Your Word says that out of the heart, the mouth speaks (Matthew 12:34). So, Lord, I pray You would reveal to me what my mind has been meditating on that would cause such ugliness to come forth. Whatever it is, please give me the strength and the self-discipline to remove its toxic influence and replace it with things that are true, wholesome, pure, lovely, admirable, and praiseworthy (Philippians 4:8).

Unhealthy Fixations

Lord, I confess that [thing I am obsessing over] is starting to have too much mastery over my life. It's what I think about, plan around; it determines my mood. Lord, *nothing* should have that kind of power over me. I'll call it what it is: an idol. An addiction. Something I am putting my trust in more than You. Forgive me for bowing my heart to another.

[Thing] is not easy to give up, but I ask You to kill my desire for it. You have called me to die to myself and to live for You. You have called me to repent and to turn from my sins and take up my cross of obedience. Please help me; I'm scared of letting go of this. What if life is as miserable without it as I imagine? No. I refuse to be mastered by [thing]. I will not be a slave to anything but righteousness (Romans 6:15-23).

Prayer over Habitual Sin

Lord, I keep returning to [habitual sin]. The things I know I *shouldn't* do are the things I keep doing. And the things that I know I *should* do I struggle to do (Romans 7:15-24). Please rescue me from my flesh, which wages war against my soul (1 Peter 2:11).

Something keeps drawing me to [habitual sin]—lying to me, telling me that [sin] is more satisfying than You. I won't ever stop the fight between myself and [habitual sin] but I will change my prayer: Oh God, help me see Your beauty, glory, and majesty. Overwhelm me with Your holiness, love, and righteousness. I beg You to reveal Yourself to my heart and mind in a way that transforms my affections. I cannot manage this by willpower. I must be drawn to something else even more. Oh my God, draw me to You more than I'm drawn to [habitual sin], and heal my broken heart.

When I'm Too Comfortable with a Shallow Faith

Lord, try as I might to have this relationship with You, I still find myself knowing more *about* You than *knowing You* personally. It's like being in a fan club: all the facts and none of the closeness. God, I don't feel like I have that intimacy that comes from truly knowing You. Sometimes I have the right head knowledge. Other times I'm complacent with worshipping a version of You that may or may not correspond to the God of Scripture. Or I substitute actual Bible study and instead pick and choose my favorite happy verses that tell me things I already want to hear, ignoring the parts of Scripture that make me uncomfortable.

I want to know You, all of You, even the parts that are difficult to understand. Right now, I picture myself meeting You face-to-face one day, and the interaction includes a stiff handshake with a "nice to finally meet You in person." I don't want it to be like that. I want it to be like meeting a cherished friend to whom I've spent a lifetime pouring out my heart. I want to run to

Your arms, confident that I knew the real You while I was here on earth. Lord, please make my walk with You more personal. May my knowledge *of* You and my relationship *with* You never outpace each other.

Lord, I don't care what You have to do to show me who You are. And yes, I realize this is a dangerous prayer to pray. When I am truly abiding in You, the cares and sufferings of this world fade away. Give me strength to withstand the training and discipline that will mold me into Your image.

When I Don't Understand Prayer

Lord, if I really understood what happened during prayer, I'd be praying without ceasing (1 Thessalonians 5:17). But I honestly don't quite understand it; *I want to, though*. Please teach me.

I pray for faith, to trust You are moving even when I cannot see You. I know it's not just about the words I say. Otherwise, You wouldn't have given us the Lord's Prayer: simple, beautiful, instructive. But in the Gospels, Jesus disappeared for days to be alone with the Father in prayer. What were You saying, Jesus? How were You asking? Surely, the God who raised You from the dead can teach me to converse with Him!

Jesus, I pray You would break down the judgmental voice in my head that tells me I'm not good at prayer. Allow my words to flow unhindered. Thank You, Lord, for welcoming my prayers no matter how feeble they are. You are such a kind teacher.

When I Feel Like I Have Let God Down

God, I feel like I am constantly letting You down. My prayers have a theme. I come and confess the same things over and over. I struggle with recurring emotions. But then I look at Your Word: "For if, while we were God's enemies, we were reconciled to him through the death of his Son, how much more, having been reconciled, shall we be saved through his life!" (Romans 5:10).

Lord, You wooed me with Your unfailing love. That love was made available to me while I was still an enemy. What in the world makes me think You are constantly disappointed or angry with me now that I'm Your child? How much more pleased are You with me now as Your daughter than You were when I was a rebel? Lord, I reject the lies of the enemy that take my own self-judgment and project it onto You. I again submit myself to Your lordship, knowing that becoming like You through sanctification is a difficult process. I doubt I'll ever have a day when I don't have to submit some aspect of myself to Your perfect law of love, which casts out fear (1 John 4:18).

I refuse to allow the enemy's condemning words to beat me into submission to my sin. And I refuse to allow his hiss of condemnation to prevent me from pursuing You. I reject shame. I reject unhealthy striving. I release my imperfections and start afresh. I reject complacency and condemnation, for "there is now no condemnation for those who are in Christ Jesus" (Romans 8:1). I am resolved: "Forgetting what is behind and straining on toward what is ahead, I press on toward the goal to win the prize for which God has called me heavenward in Christ Jesus" (Philippians 3:13-14).

Section 9

WHEN. I. JUST. CAN'T. EVEN.

Courage for Being Misunderstood as a Christian

Lord, I know it shouldn't bother me, but I care about what other people think of me. I know that in other parts of the world, people are severely persecuted for the sake of Your name. They are willing and even called to lay down their very lives for You. My struggles have much smaller consequences, but those consequences still sting. Here I am, trying to be obedient to You—to lovingly but honestly speak truth into cultural issues—and I am laughed at. People think I'm either crazy or heartless. No matter how respectful I try to be, they are offended. They accuse me of hate, even as they hate me. I need Your courage. I want to please You more than man (Galatians 1:10). But my fear of backlash and vitriol is also real.

I'm scared of being snubbed by friends and family because I spoke truth. Lord, so many relationships are changing. Tension that wasn't there before now exists with people in my life. Following You is starting to cost more. I'm afraid it's going to get worse. I need

Your help to model courage for my little bears, because they are going to need it. Help me model Your heart so they know Your praise is worth more than any worldly approval they might have to give up. Help me equip them to stand on and for Your truth while still loving like Jesus. Help me inspire them to persevere and endure, even when following You is hard. Even when it hurts. Even when it's scary. Even when it's lonely. My prayer for my family is that we would be strong and courageous because You are with us when we follow You (Joshua 1:9). You will not leave us or forsake us (Deuteronomy 31:6). Please strengthen us, help us, and uphold us. Teach us to fear not (Isaiah 41:10).

Longing for Justice in an Unjust World

Heavenly Father, it grieves me to see wickedness increase in Your perfectly created world. Things seem to get worse with each passing day because we've abandoned Your truth and moral law. What You called good in the beginning is now called evil, and what is evil is now called good. Horrible acts of violence are committed against the most vulnerable image bearers. People mock You without suffering consequences for their actions. In my limited understanding, I can't comprehend why You allow humans to go unpunished after committing such atrocious acts.

What I do know is that You are good, and Your Word is true. In the end, You will do what is right. Psalm 89:14 says, "Righteousness and justice are the foundation of Your throne; love and faithfulness go before You." And Your Word confirms to me that You will not overlook injustice in the world forever. I am confident You are also able to use the evil deeds of wicked people to accomplish Your perfect plan.

If I'm being honest, each sin I commit against one of my fellow image bearers—out of jealousy, selfishness, rage, or bitterness—is really against You, my holy God. I often fail to love people the way You have commanded, and that is rebellious and wrong. With the psalmist I confess that I have sinned against You alone, so You are right when You pass sentence and judge me (Psalm 51:4). Please create in me a clean heart and renew a steadfast spirit within me as I come before You in brokenness and humility (Psalm 51:10, 17).

Thank You for providing an advocate in Jesus, who is perfectly righteous and comes before You on my behalf. Lord, I long for the day when You will restore all things and make everything as it should be once again. Until then, help me to trust Your perfect plan.

74

Loving like Jesus When the World Has Redefined Love

Lord, You say in Your Word to love You with all my heart, soul, mind, and strength, and to love others as myself (Mark 12:30-31). You tell us that the world will know we are Christians by our love (John 13:35). My children want to love like Jesus loved, loving the unlovable and being a champion for those who are suffering. But how can I teach them what true love *is* when the world's definition is so different?

Teach me to model true love. May I be patient without enabling. May I be kind without compromising truth. May I not envy what others have, and may I never flaunt what I have to tempt others to envy me. When I am annoyed, may I counter it with Your grace. May I seek Your best for others even *more* than they do for themselves.

When the world tells me it is "loving" while embracing lies, may I refuse to participate, even when I am called names for doing so. God, You are the way, the truth, and the life, and Your Word is truth (John 14:6;

17:17). May I rejoice whenever I see truth being proclaimed and help others to see the beauty of that truth.

Remind me that nobody is beyond Your grace. May I always point people to the glory that awaits them despite the hardships of this world, and may I encourage those enduring hardships by helping carry their burdens (Galatians 6:2). Help me endure the sorrows of this world, knowing that endurance produces perseverance, which produces character, which produces hope for the glory to come—and that hope will never disappoint (Romans 5:3-5). Your love never ends. When I feel tempted to compromise, direct me back to Your definition of love (1 Corinthians 13:4-8).

When My Kids Are So Loud, Needy, and Whiny That I Want to Scream

God, I feel like I am the deputy director of a million stupid things that I couldn't care less about, but which seem to determine whether my kids will have a meltdown or not. I cannot handle the whining. I cannot handle the screaming. I cannot handle the snot and the tears and their endless clawing at me for more, more, more. More of me when I feel like I am spent. I've got nothing left. How does any of this matter in the eternal scheme of things? I am exhausted all the time, and I can't point to a single thing I accomplished today that feels meaningful.

I need You, God, because I am about to lose it. So I choose right now to shut my mouth, quiet my heart, and return to what is true. All of this matters because my children matter. These thousands of tiny sacrifices are reinforcing in them that they have a mother who cares about what matters to them. And I pray that my caring about their little things will one day translate into knowing that *You* care about the little things. All the things. So, for that reason, I will never stop caring. I will never stop giving. I will never stop doing the job You have called me to do.

God, I choose to be still in this moment—despite their cries in the background—and meditate on this truth, reminding myself of why I do what I do. Oh Lord, You are so pleased with my every effort to love and care for these children, and Your pleasure has an eternal weight to it. All things can be done for Your glory, God. Thank You for this reminder. God, give me the energy to continue through this day, and refresh my sleep for another day of the same.

When I Want to Run Away from My Responsibilities

Oh God, I need You right now. I feel broken, bloodied, and bruised. I feel overwhelmed with too many tasks and incapable of doing them all well. My body is tired. My mind cannot focus.

I imagine myself running away from all my responsibilities, but there is no freedom in that either. Because when I stop and think about it, I love the tasks You have given me. My job, my family, my children, and all that comes with them are blessings from You. I am the one You have chosen for this role.

Your righteous right hand will uphold me (Isaiah 41:10). Oh God, plant that knowledge deep in my heart. I pray that I would feel Your strength flowing into me. And in the times when I can't feel it, I pray You would endow me with a special abundance of faith.

Am I Doing Enough?

Lord, I sometimes feel so guilty that I'm not doing enough. I'm not volunteering at homeless shelters. I'm not working at a food bank. I'm not even teaching Sunday school. I worry I'm only doing the "good works" that I feel comfortable with, and when I get to heaven, You'll ask me how I missed so much of what You said.

Thank You that I'm only held accountable for how I use the time, energy, and resources You have given me; I'm not measured against how others use what You've provided them. The day will come when I can take on more; this is just a difficult season of parenting. In the meantime, open my eyes to the needs I *can* meet. Show me things I can do with my children so that my service becomes another facet in their discipleship training. Help me give myself grace when even the load I already carry feels too heavy.

78

When I Feel like the Wrong Mom for the Job

Heavenly Father, I don't feel equipped to be a good mom today. I was too irritable, too harsh, and I just want to hide from my kids. I don't want shame to win today. You have called me to this role, which means You will equip me for it. Thank You for new mercies every morning (Lamentations 3:22-23). Thank You for the gift and calling of motherhood. Thank You for the truth that when I am weak, You are strong (2 Corinthians 12:10).

Lord, I surrender myself to You once again. Let my kids see a mama who is always reliant upon her heavenly Father. Please help me to represent You to my children by showing them Your patience, steadfastness, and grace.

Help me learn to give myself grace. My children can learn more from watching me navigate my mistakes than they would if I made motherhood look easy. So, God, I praise You even in my failures.

Praying Through Exhaustion

Dear Lord, thank You so much for the blessing of being a mother. Right now, I stand where I once only prayed to be. You in Your infinite wisdom gave me these children in Your timing, and I trust You, but I'm still struggling.

I'm afraid to even speak this out loud because I'm ashamed of how I feel. Too often, I feel like I am at my breaking point. I'm worn down by trying to raise these children well. This stage of motherhood seems beyond my strength and understanding. I feel like I'm failing before breakfast. I never knew motherhood could be so incredibly hard. Even though I love my children dearly, I wasn't prepared for the 24-7 nature of parenting. At night, I drop into bed exhausted and defeated. But I don't want to just survive these hard days. I want to thrive. I want to be known for Your peace and patience instead of my stress and anxiety. I need Your presence and encouragement to keep me from being crushed by the hamster wheel of my kids' schedules. Help me recognize when I'm taking on burdens and expectations I was never meant to carry. Please help me ignore the messages of this world, which tell me that my day is never done. May I instead dwell in Your grace and Sabbath rest.

Give me supernatural strength for the tiring moments, patience for the frustrating ones, and joy in the more monotonous tasks of homemaking and mothering. Please help me disciple my children, not just discipline them. I know You love me when I'm at my lowest just as much as my highest. Help me love my children the same way.

Remind me to be present in everyday moments. May I relish the ways motherhood is refining and growing me. Help me remember the messes and chores mean my home and heart are full.

Asking the Holy Spirit to Help Me Pray

Lord, I confess I don't know how to pray for this situation. My words don't even form; they just come out as a guttural cry, and I feel overwhelmed. It's all too much. But You have been faithful in the past, so I am asking You to be faithful again. Your Word tells me Your Holy Spirit is my helper, and when I do not know how I ought to pray, Your Spirit Himself intercedes for me (Romans 8:26). Please do that now.

Teach me to be intentional, partnering always with Your Spirit, asking for help in every situation, and bringing all requests and petitions to You. I feel so discouraged right now, but I choose to place my hope in You. May I walk closely with the Holy Spirit as I go about my day, moving forward in wisdom and clear thinking because You transform my mind (Romans 12:2).

Holy Spirit, help me in my weakness. All around me, evil seems to triumph and the wicked continue to prosper. The world I was born into no longer exists. But for my children and their children, I do not want to give up on praying, asking for what has been broken to be restored. But when my prayers feel futile and words will not come, Holy Spirit, please intercede for me. When all I have to give are tears, and when my thoughts and feelings cannot be put into human terms, thank You for giving me Your words. As I seek to remain steadfast in prayer, please continue to search my heart and guide me in lifting up this situation in accordance with the will of the Father.

When God Feels Silent

Father, I'm praying but I hear nothing. I feel nothing. I know that You aren't ignoring me; You know the number of hairs on my head (Luke 12:7). So why can't I hear You?

Could it be that my ears have grown so accustomed to the manic noise of this world that I have dulled my ability to hear from You? As I squirm in the silence, I am reminded to cease my striving and be still before You (Psalm 46:10). Your silence is not from lack of attention. I may not hear You, Lord, but You have not forgotten me.

When Your silence feels unbearable, may Your calming hand soothe my ever-active brain. When I feel like I can do anything but be still, may You provide ways to foster stillness. Please give me the self-control and patience to wait on Your voice when it doesn't feel like it's coming fast enough.

God, Please Use a Megaphone

God, the Bible tells us that You sometimes speak in a still small voice—that You aren't necessarily in the tornadoes, the rainstorms, the lightning, or the hail. At times, You are the quiet whisper (1 Kings 19:11-12). But honestly, with the noise and the chaos of little kids running around and everything else going on, I can't hear any whispers. I'm really going to need that giant megaphone voice from heaven telling me, "Do this!" or "Do that!"

I need clear direction. I need clear guidance. And yet I know Your will isn't always just one thing. So Lord, bring me the wisdom of Your Word, godly counsel, and the knowledge of when I have the freedom to move ahead in a variety of directions as long as I'm within the latitude of Your moral will. You delight in our decisions, so please keep me from making a really dumb one. Nail doors shut if they need to be shut. And if a door needs to be opened, Lord...use dynamite to blow that sucker open.

I want to hear You more clearly. I want to do Your will, but so often I feel like I'm blindly stumbling along and hoping to be in the general vicinity of the right path. Yet You say You give wisdom "generously to all without finding fault" (James 1:5). Please help me hear You in whatever way You choose to speak, trusting that even when it feels like a guessing game, I hear You more than I realize. In hindsight, I can often tell where Your hand was at work and where You guided me, but I need a little extra hand-holding right now. I trust that I'll look back and see Your providence and goodness during this time as well.

When My Anxiety About the World Rubs Off on My Child

Dear God, I'm anxious about the state of our world, and it's rubbing off on my kids. Every day I read more bad news, more stories that sicken or anger me, and they put me in a funk. I vocalize my concerns to my husband while little ears are listening, which often is not wise. My kids are not growing up in the same kind of world I did, and they know it. It worries them, Lord, and it worries me too.

Please give me wisdom to navigate this "new" world with my kids. I know You give wisdom to those who ask, Lord, and oh, how I need it (James 1:5)! Help me also to hold my tongue when I'm around my children so as to not worry them with things too great for their little hearts to bear (Proverbs 21:23). Turn me away from my phone and television and instead to Your Word (Psalm 119:28). Give me peace, calmness, and confidence that You are on Your throne, in complete control (Psalm 103:19). Help me to not be anxious about tomorrow, next week, or next year, and may the peace that overcomes me wash over my kids too (Philippians 4:6-7). I don't want them to be anxious, Lord, so please calm my anxious heart. And in those times when my children's anxiety isn't secondhand, when the world itself overwhelms them and tries to steal their joy, make them resilient, faithful, and strong. I trust You, Lord, with the hearts of my children.

When I Can't Focus on My Bible Reading

Father, I'm sitting here trying to get into the Word, but my mind keeps going in a million different directions. It's like my brain is working on overdrive, trying to find something (anything!) else to do. I don't understand it. *Why* is this such a battle?

There are so many times when I walk away from Your Word feeling refreshed, refilled, and ready to conquer the day. And then there are days like today…when reading Your Word feels like a total chore. I didn't hear anything specific, and I don't feel like I've learned anything in particular. It is just a check mark on my to-do list. I know not every Bible reading will offer some huge epiphany, but neither is every meal I eat a culinary masterpiece. Nourishment is nourishment, even if I don't feel it immediately.

When I am distracted, delete those thoughts from my head. When I am unfocused, draw me back in. Even when reading Scripture just feels like a duty, may I delight in the obedience of the act and feel Your pleasure at my perseverance. And may I remember that just because I don't feel "changed" doesn't mean I am *not* changed by this small act of faithfulness. Lord, please give me an insatiable craving for the Word. I cannot change my own heart or desires, but You can. I thank You for delighting in my attempts, no matter how feeble.

Section 10

MIND, BODY, AND EMOTIONS

Healthy Attitude Toward My Body

Lord, I pray for my body and the way I steward it. Help me remember that my body is not a gift to be done with as I see fit, but a resource for which I am accountable.

I pray I would not look down on my body for all the things I wish it were, but that I would love and care for it instead. Lord, please help me replace the criticism I've spoken over my body with words that elevate this wonderful blessing You've given me to steward. May I never see the needs of my body as being at war with the needs of my spirit. You have made me body, soul, mind, and spirit. May I cultivate this body for my good, and to the glory of the One who gave it to me.

Lord, there are things I can do to take care of my body, but there are also things I cannot change. Please give me a right and healthy attitude in how I interact with my body—treating it with neither scorn nor pride. Please remind me what is within my power to change and what is not. I pray that I would not try to force it to do what it cannot do, but that I would lovingly develop it to do more than what I thought possible. As I age, help me to accept the parts that sag, dribble, and pucker. Help me to accept the natural process of aging without fear.

God, thank You for my body. I especially thank You for [part of my body that I am often ungrateful for]. Thank You for how You knit me together, and I thank You that all parts of me that are not working well will be made whole again. But until that day comes, may I never stop giving thanks for what I have.

Taming Emotions

Lord, emotions can be helpful. But sometimes my emotions can be all noise and no information.

God, I pray for the ability to separate feeling from fact, reason from emotion. Not once in Your Word do You command us to *feel* something. We are commanded to *be* and we are commanded to *do*. I pray You would help me take control over what I can control and empower me to react maturely based on what I know, not impulsively based on how I feel in the moment.

Thank You for how emotions help me when they are properly disciplined by Scripture, reason, and reality. I thank You for how they spur me toward defending the defenseless and speaking out against injustice. Please show me when my feelings reflect things that aren't true. May I always have the humility to correct myself and apologize when my passions overtake my ability to reason with godly wisdom.

When My Brain Needs to Slow the Heck Down

It is so hard for me to be still right now, God. My mind is moving in a thousand different directions at once. You call us to be still and to wait patiently for You, no matter what is going on in the world around us (Psalm 37:7). So please take this meager sacrifice of stillness and use it to refocus me on trusting and delighting in You.

[Take a deep breath between each statement.]
You call us to be still and know that You are God (Psalm 46:10).
I sit here in stillness, Lord, as an act of obedience.
Being still before You is an act of worship.
I choose to focus on You in this moment, God.
You are the truth, so I turn my thoughts to You (John 14:6).
Lord, You are good. Release my desire for control.
Lord, You are peace, so I rest in Your presence.
Your presence is beautiful and worth slowing down for.

Lord, You are trustworthy and wise (Romans 11:33).
I will not miss out on anything that matters by being still in Your presence.
You will bring to mind the things I need to remember.
You are sovereign over what is stressing me out right now (Ephesians 4:6).
You have seen everything that is going to happen from beginning to end (Isaiah 46:10).
I can rest in Your provision and sovereignty.
I can rest in Your goodness (Psalm 145:9).
Lord, protect me from the noise.

General Healing

Lord, You are the Great Physician, and I pray for physical healing over [person] right now. Please put Your hand on [person]. I know You are able and willing, Lord (Luke 5:13), but we live in a fallen world, so we may not see healing this side of eternity. I thank You for inviting us to pester You in prayer, like the widow begging for justice (Luke 18:1-5). So I pray with eager expectation, even while releasing the results to You.

If the treatment is uncomfortable, I pray You would carry [person] through this difficult season. Please take away the pain in this moment as we await Your healing, whether natural or supernatural. May those around [him/her] give [him/her] grace while [he/she] is ailing. Above all, give [person] peace while [his/her] body is hurting. May [he/she] find purpose in this pain, knowing You can use all things toward good for those who love You (Romans 8:28).

Anxiety-Ridden Child

Lord, please give me the wisdom to be a mother to a child with anxiety. When peace evades my child, give [him/her] the peace that exists only in Your presence. Let Your hope pour from my lips, giving [him/her] reasons to be calm. Let me be tender and compassionate when [his/her] body is reacting outside of [his/her] control.

Please give me a place of respite where I can secretly cry out to You without [him/her] seeing the additional burdens [his/her] anxiety causes for me. When I can't handle the stress of [his/her] emotional outpourings, give me a healthy release and transform me into a tangible reflection of Your gentleness who can help soothe [his/her] anxious mind. Carry me, Lord, when my energy doesn't match what is required to face the challenges [his/her] struggles bring. Sustain me when I run on no sleep night after night because [child] is waking me up like a newborn baby. Let [child] see me casting my cares upon You so that [he/she] knows [he/she] can do the same. Help me to not make [him/her] feel like a burden.

Do not let this anxiety strangle the joy out of our days and our relationship. Teach me to communicate with [child] in a way that doesn't demean [his/her] worries or make [him/her] feel guilty. Give me words to de-escalate [his/her] emotions when [his/her] brain is holding [him/her] captive. Help me understand [his/her] limitations yet challenge [him/her] to move past them. I'd ask for You to give me patience, but I suspect that is what You're already doing. This *is* Your training ground. Fill me with Your grace and wisdom until they become permanent parts of my character, not just temporarily borrowed pieces from Yours. I can't do this alone. Help me to feel Your presence as I seek to be a calming presence for my child.

Section 11

CHURCH, STATE, SCHOOL, AND CULTURE

For Our Churches to Become Healthier

Lord, I pray over our church, its pastors, and its leadership. I know our leaders feel the pressure to be good representatives of Christ, especially with so much damage being done in Your name. God, we want to be a people who love and invite other sinners into our midst—all of us are beggars looking for the Bread of Life. But I am worried that too many churches are sacrificing Your eternal Word for the sake of aligning with the world's definition of love. God, I pray for Your church, Your bride. Please raise up leaders, watchmen on the wall, who will protect the flock from savage wolves (Isaiah 62:6; Acts 20:29-31). Increase our church's brotherly affection toward one another, and let honest rebuke become an extension of that love (Proverbs 27:5). Expose those who seek to water down Your commands and teach others to do the same (Matthew 5:19).

Show us how to model healthy church discipline: not seeking to shame people into submission but loving the body of Christ enough to uphold righteousness because sin, unchecked, spreads like wildfire through a congregation. Lord, our culture has seen church discipline done in harmful and abusive ways. I pray for Your wisdom on how to purify Your bride without putting loads on people's backs that are too heavy to bear (Matthew 23:4). Protect us from being a church whose love makes people complacent with sin, or whose truth lacks kindness. You say the road to You is narrow. Please help us walk this narrow line between love and truth, and have the wisdom to know what approach is most appropriate in each specific situation. I release any feelings of angst where I am taking too much responsibility into my own hands. I thank You for being our Good Shepherd.

For Unity and Division

Lord, we are such a divided people, even within the church. As long as it depends on us, we are to live at peace with all people (1 Corinthians 1:10; Romans 12:18). But the one time You have not called us to peace is when lies are spoken as truths or evil is called good. We are living in a society that sees all disagreement as hate, but we are to love what You love and to hate what You hate (Psalm 45:7)! So, Lord, we pray for a godly unity around that which is righteous, and a godly division from anything that wages war against our souls or is raised against the knowledge of You (1 Peter 2:11; 2 Corinthians 10:5). I pray that I would be willing to divide over things that matter, so please give me the wisdom to know what really matters. I pray for the church, that You would sift the wheat from the chaff. I pray that those who love You would be willing to be hated on account of You. But I pray we would be hated for standing up for truth, not for being obnoxious with that truth.

God, show us where we are dividing over convictions, not commands. Show us where we are separating over emphases, not essentials. And God, where we are embracing folly and wickedness, may we repent and be willing to divide for the health of the church. It is so hard to know when our love is supposed to cover a multitude of sins and when compromise is polluting our fellowship (1 Peter 4:8; Revelation 2:20; 1 Corinthians 5:9-13). God, give us wisdom. Increase the unity within our ranks by increasing the knowledge of what You have called us to be as Christians. Lord, make me an instrument of Your peace, but never at the expense of holiness.

For Biblically Minded Teachers and Administrators in Public School

Lord, we pray for the public schools where Your name is not allowed to be openly proclaimed. Raise up God-fearing administrators into leadership roles. Grant them favor among their peers, students, and the parents. May the fragrance of Christ permeate their demeanor, competence, and knowledge and attract others to You.

Shield both teachers and administrators from the pressures of a culture that prioritizes feelings over facts and politeness over goodness. Remind teachers that they can teach Your truth without having to cite the Bible, because all truth is Your truth. Deafen their ears when the enemy encourages them to question what You have said in Your Word, and may they be able to artfully incorporate Your truth into each academic discipline in a way that displays common sense. May their teaching refute the idea that students can create their own truth or construct their own reality. And empower administrators to choose curriculum and teachers that promote this truth.

May the staff be faithful employees with stellar reputations so no false accusations raised against them can stand. May their words be true but seasoned with salt and fitting for the moment. Give them patience and gentleness when needed, but firmness and conviction as well. May they never tire of doing the right thing even when it is not popular. Show them when they must disobey man in order to obey God, and provide for them financially if their decisions result in termination. May they have the courage to take that chance, knowing that obeying You will sometimes disqualify them in the secular world. As people of God, please let their classrooms or offices be places where Your presence is felt. Use them as ambassadors for Your kingdom as they steward the gifts and the positions You have given them.

Protection for Teachers Who Refuse to Teach Lies

God, we pray for the educators who are being pressured to teach ideologies that contradict reality or deny Your created order. Show them where they do and do not have academic freedom to teach about the Bible and Christianity with regard to history, culture, and values.

Where lies are being taught, where reality is called false, where evil is called good, we plead for Your intervention. Empower teachers to hold their ground even when pressured to conform. Help them be willing to sacrifice their own reputations (and even their jobs!) for the sake of protecting the hearts and minds of children. Bring administrators, peers, families, and church communities alongside them in support.

Protect these brave teachers from manipulation, deception, and marginalization. May their refusal to teach lies embolden others to do the same. Raise up common sense in our land, and tear down the strongholds choking the truth out of our schools.

Protection over Freedom of Speech and Religion in Schools

Lord, we are not guaranteed any rights on this side of eternity but we thank You for how You provided for Americans anyway—inspiring our forefathers to codify the Bill of Rights into our Constitution. These "inalienable rights," however, are coming under attack, and we ask they be upheld in our schools. We ask especially for Your protection over freedom of speech and freedom of religion. May no secret or public agenda be allowed to tear these rights down.

We pray that our public schools and universities would respect and honor our right to speak truth and worship You. Protect our students' and faculty's right to graciously express their beliefs on campus even if they are labeled hateful. May unconstitutional restrictions on speaking freely about critical issues be removed. Protect the rights of student clubs and campus ministries to freely associate. Expose hypocrisy where double standards prevent Christians from speaking while posing no restrictions on their secular counterparts. But also expose the hypocrisy when Christians deny others this same right.

May our students seek to obey the laws of the land, but also let them resist the temptation to trade biblical authority for governmental authority. Help them stand against the pressure to only express thoughts or feelings that align with the secular narrative. When they must speak up, may they make grace-filled arguments that cannot be refuted.

As being a Christian becomes more difficult, train our children to consider the cost of following You. May they count it as a privilege. Let nothing harass them into silence. As Paul invoked his rights as a Roman citizen, may our children be courageous enough to stand up for the rights afforded them under our Constitution (Acts 22:24-28). Let these rights be fairly applied to all—Christian and non-Christian alike.

95

When My Child Is Bullied

Lord, I pray for [child] and [his/her] sense of self when other kids pick out [his/her] insecurities and bully [him/her]. May [child] stand up for [himself/herself] in an appropriate manner, and may those in authority take swift action to stop this mistreatment. May the other kids who witness this behavior also speak up on [child's] behalf.

I pray for [child's] strength to follow Your example, Jesus, loving [his/her] enemies by praying for [the bully] instead of seeking revenge. Where the bully is reacting from hurt, insecurity, or instability, may my child have the eyes to see the root cause and the compassion to speak life. I pray for [child] to be able to see a heart that is hurting so badly it needs to cause pain in others. Where the bullying stems from anger, arrogance, or childish vindictiveness, may you humble [him/her] in a way that silences [his/her] pride. Remove whatever pedestal this bully is standing on that makes [him/her] feel superior to others; provide authorities who will put the bully in [his/her] place without crushing [his/her] spirit. Please nip this instinct to bully in the bud.

God, give me the wisdom to know how to act. Make it clear when I need to be a Mama Bear, and give me the discernment and peace to address this situation well when I feel like marching in and giving this bully a taste of [his/her] own medicine. Help me balance the desire to protect my child with the courage to let [him/her] figure out how to fight [his/her] own battles. There will come a day when I can't protect [child], but right now, God, give me wisdom in how to respond, how to protect, and how to allow You to build [child's] character. There are a thousand and one ways to do this wrong. Lord, be my guide in this situation.

When My Child Is the Bully

Lord, please bring to my attention if or when my child is being a bully. I pray for the humility to recognize that my child is not incapable of bullying, and for the courage to take appropriate disciplinary measures.

Give me insight as I seek to discern the root cause. Reveal to me if my child is compensating for feelings of powerlessness in another situation, and help me advocate for [him/her] so that [he/she] doesn't compensate this way. If my child's self-esteem has risen dangerously high, may I help [him/her] see [himself/herself] accurately. Please reveal [child's] weaknesses and insecurities to [him/her] and then use that knowledge to cultivate compassion for others. Help me teach [him/her] to use [his/her] strength, beauty, popularity, or any other gifts for protecting those around [him/her], not for being top dog.

Lord, where the bullying was accidental, I pray You would show [child] how to use [his/her] words more carefully and how to be aware of when [his/her] actions are causing another child to feel unsafe or insecure. Lord, I pray You would remove [child's] pride without removing [his/her] spunk. May this be a phase that [he/she] grows out of, and one we can use to shape [his/her] character for the future. Where our family is guilty of modeling this behavior in our home, help us grow in gentleness so we can once again show [child] how to be strong and funny without being hurtful.

I pray that we as parents of the bully and the bullied would be a unified front. May we not be dragged into the drama of our kids. Let us see ourselves as being on the same team to eradicate this behavior no matter whose child is responsible. Thank You, Lord, for bringing this behavior to light so we can work to stop this cycle before [child] becomes an adult.

Atmosphere in the Traditional Classroom

Lord, I pray for the atmosphere in my child's classroom. I pray for [teacher's] passion for the academic content, that [teacher] would be so excited about these topics that the students can't help but get excited as well. I pray for them to experience a genuine enjoyment of learning, and for You to protect the class from the students with an "I couldn't care less" attitude that ruins the learning environment for everyone. I pray against any behavioral problems; when the students enter the classroom, please fill them with an overwhelming sense of calm. I pray for [teacher's] ability to redirect problem behavior and to manage the classroom so that one child's behavior doesn't dictate the tone for the rest. I pray against anyone—student or adult—who would put the other students in danger; please, God, thwart any plans for harm and keep the classroom a safe place.

May Your peace be present among all students; allow them to leave any problems happening in their homes outside the doors so they can focus on becoming well-rounded, intelligent, knowledgeable, truthful, and kind human beings. I pray You would protect the class from rivalries and cliques; instead, allow the students to enjoy each other, appreciating one another's gifts, talents, and quirks. I pray the class would have a team atmosphere with each student cheering on their peers, engaging in healthy competition without vying for dominance. Thank You for being the God who created math, science, language, and art. Restore my students' and their classmates' childlike wonder as they learn about Your world.

Atmosphere While Homeschooling

Lord, You have called us to homeschool, but some days it is so hard. Please remind me that this journey belongs to You. Help me dedicate my time and effort to Your glory, for Your purposes, and to lay down my agenda for each day. Give me a heart to disciple my children as we walk through all facets of their education.

For me as their teacher, I pray that I will earn and keep their respect—that just because I am their mom, they will not neglect to form habits of diligence and excellence. Help me speak only what edifies and encourages, disciplining from love, not from anger or frustration. When preparation and teaching get tough, help me to demonstrate a healthy balance of working hard and resting well.

Please help me foster teachable spirits that desire to learn. Help my children cultivate focus by not giving in to distraction. When tensions get high, protect them from jealous or quarrelsome attitudes toward one another. Grant me the ability to love and nurture my children, recognizing their unique needs, skills, and weaknesses. Create in them a desire to glorify You in their schoolwork and lives.

Let us never make learning differences an excuse for not trying our best. When we deal with those differences and their inherent struggles, may we not see them as obstacles but as springboards for overcoming challenges and improving character.

I pray, Lord, that my children will look back on homeschooling with fondness, remembering it as a time of family bonding and excellent academic preparation for life. Father, make our classroom a place that shines the light of the gospel and trains our children to go out into the world equipped with Your wisdom, prepared to stand tall in the darkness.

Child's Ability to Learn/ Learning Disabilities

Lord, I pray for [child] and [his/her] time at school. Lord, [area of struggle] is so difficult for [him/her]. My child did not choose this hardship. But You have chosen me to be [his/her] mom. I accept it and I accept [him/her]—struggles and all.

Please reach into [child's] mind where things aren't connecting and give [him/her] the ability to absorb what is being taught. Where there is stubbornness, show me exactly how hard to push, knowing You push me to do difficult things without pushing so hard that I break. Help us learn to balance acceptance and striving. This will not be the last difficult thing [child] experiences in life, Lord, so I ask that this be a learning opportunity in persistence.

If needed, please provide us with a correct diagnosis and treatment. Give us doctors and counselors who see my child as a soul and not a label. Give us thick skin, a soft heart, and a sound mind. Please guide [child's] teachers' words; may they praise [his/

her] sincere efforts without comparing [him/her] to other kids.

Help [child] continue to experience enough progress that [he/she] knows [he/she] is able and capable to overcome whatever challenge this learning difference throws at [him/her]. Lord, I pray You would remove from [him/her] the burden to reach a certain level, but at the same time, help [him/her] take responsibility for what [he/she] *is* capable of.

Lord, give us a support group that has already walked this road so they can help us navigate and provide hope for the journey. Thank You for how You've created us all to think differently, because sharing our unique perspectives allows each of us to see what we would be blind to on our own. Remind [child] that what feels like a challenge right now will one day be used to make [him/her] excellent at what You've called [him/her] to do.

Ending Prayer:

Creating a Legacy of Prayer

Julie Loos

Lord, thank You that we are surrounded by such a great cloud of witnesses. That hall of faith in Hebrews 11 demonstrates what Your people have accomplished by faith.

For those of us with a godly legacy, we thank You for family members before us who walked obediently, prayed faithfully, and left footsteps for us to follow. May we take their baton and run with endurance until we're called to pass it on. May those behind us become the spiritual marathon runners of the future.

For those of us without that legacy, empower us to become prayer pioneers in our families. We know and proclaim: "Let us run with perseverance the race marked out for us, fixing our eyes on Jesus, the pioneer and perfecter of faith" (Hebrews 12:1-2). We ask You to help us leave a legacy of faith supported by prayer. May it be for our descendants' good and for Your glory.

Answered Prayer Requests

Answered Prayer Requests

Scripture Versions Used

To learn more about Harvest House books and to read sample chapters, visit our website:

www.HarvestHousePublishers.com